Samurai
Weapons

Samurai
Weapons

TOOLS OF
THE WARRIOR

Don Cunningham

TUTTLE PUBLISHING
Tokyo • Rutland, Vermont • Singapore

Published by Tuttle Publishing, an imprint of Periplus Editions (HK) Ltd., with editorial offices at 364 Innovation Drive, North Clarendon, Vermont 05759 U.S.A.

Copyright © 2008 Don Cunningham

Library of Congress Cataloging-in-Publication Data

Cunningham, Don (Don A.)
  Samurai weapons : tools of the warrior / Don Cunningham.
     p. cm.
  Includes bibliographical references and index.
  ISBN 978-4-8053-0958-2 (pbk.: alk. paper)
1. Martial arts weapons--Japan--history. 2. Samurai. 3. Weapons--Japan--History.
  I. Title.
U821.J3C86 2008
952'.02--dc22

2007020864

ISBN-10: 4-8053-0958-X
ISBN-13: 978-4-8053-0958-2

Distributed by

North America, Latin America & Europe	*Japan*	*Asia Pacific*
Tuttle Publishing	Tuttle Publishing	Berkeley Books Pte. Ltd
364 Innovation Drive	Yaekari Building, 3rd Floor	61 Tai Seng Avenue #02-12
North Clarendon,	5-4-12 Osaki	Singapore 534167
VT 05759-9436 U.S.A.	Shinagawa-ku	Tel: (65) 6280-3320
Tel: 1 (802) 773-8930	Tokyo 141 0032	Fax: (65) 6280-6290
Fax: 1 (802) 773-6993	Tel: (81) 3 5437-0171	inquiries@periplus.com.sg
info@tuttlepublishing.com	Fax: (81) 3 5437-0755	www.periplus.com
www.tuttlepublishing.com	tuttle-sales@gol.com	

First edition
12 11 10 09 08 07   10 9 8 7 6 5 4 3 2 1

Printed in Singapore

Frontispiece: In this print by Ichiyusai Kunitoshi, two feudal police officers use a jutte and chains during an attempt to arrest the famous robber Inuzuka Shinao.

TUTTLE PUBLISHING® is a registered trademark of Tuttle Publishing, a division of Periplus Editions (HK) Ltd.

In memory of Nawa Yumio (1912–2006),
the last sōke of Masaki-ryū Manrikigusari-jutsu and
Edo Machikata Jutte-jutsu. Thank you for sharing your insights
and details unavailable from any other source about feudal-era
arresting implements and procedures.

For Robert Gruzanski,
son of Charles Gruzanski (1933–1972),
author of *Spike and Chain: Japanese Fighting Arts*
and inspiration for my study of feudal Japanese martial arts history.
Thank you for sharing memories of your father
and his contributions to the martial arts.

Contents

Preface

One of the benefits of working for a Japanese telecommunications manufacturer was the frequency of opportunities to continue my study of Kodokan Judo in the country where this remarkable martial art originated. Practicing judo at local Japanese judo dojos and participating in the frequent tournament competitions after work and on weekends, I gained many friends who shared my interest in judo as well as in other Japanese martial arts. I also took up kendo, or the Japanese art of fencing with bamboo swords. The etiquette and practice of kendo is strongly influenced by traditions dating back to the classical Japanese martial art styles. Because of this, I became fascinated with Japan's martial arts culture and wanted to learn as much as I could about the samurai and their ancient traditions. After reading as much as possible about Japanese history and weaponry and seeking out the very few schools which still taught Japanese swordsmanship in the ancient combat styles, I became particularly interested in jujutsu, the unarmed fighting styles.

For entertainment and partly to further develop my limited language skills, I would often watch *jidai-geki* (period dramas) on Japanese television. A popular genre of both Japanese television and film—and sometimes referred to as *chambara*, a word representing the sound of clashing swords—jidai-geki retells old legends, recreates epic historical events, and in general honors the samurai spirit. Rooted in the early traditions of Japan's kabuki and nō theater arts, jidai-geki are most frequently set during the Edo period, Japan's feudal era (1603–1867), and usually feature lots of samurai swordplay and simple themes whereby the evil are punished and the good are rewarded.

While surfing channels in my Japanese hotel room one afternoon, I came across a jidai-geki series featuring Zenigata Heiji, a one-of-a-kind character. Heiji was a *goyōkiki,* basically a poor non-samurai assistant working for the higher ranking police officials in Edo. He solved crimes based more on investigation than brute force. Since he was not a member of the samurai class, Heiji was forbidden by law to wear a sword or carry a bladed weapon. To compensate for this limitation, Heiji displayed a remarkable ability to throw heavy coins like bullets, to disarm and capture criminals. He also was armed with a strange-looking iron truncheon, called a jutte, which he used to disarm his opponents without bloodshed. Although the coin throwing skill was obviously a writer's invention, I noticed that many feudal era police characters in other jidai-geki were also armed with jutte.

I frequently trained at Asahi Judo Academy during my stays in Japan. Located in Higashi-Hakuraku district near the center of Yokohama, the dojo is well known as one of the top judo schools for junior and senior high school competitors. The head instructor, Asahi Dai sensei, was also the judo instructor for the Kanagawa Prefecture Police Department, so many of the local officers practiced there as well in the evenings. Learning of my interest in the jutte, several of my police friends eagerly demonstrated the many different disarming and restraining techniques using the implement. Although modern Japanese police no longer carry a jutte, they are armed with a similar spring-loaded baton called a keibo. The keibo is often employed in their practice of modern taiho-jutsu, "body restraining" or "arresting art," which is mandatory training for most of the regular police officers. I learned that many of the jutte techniques from ancient martial arts styles were the basis for current keibo techniques.

In my search for more information, I discovered the samurai employed a wide range of weaponry other than the sword, bow, and spear. Many of these were used for self-defense in places where swords were not allowed or as alternatives for situations in which the use of swords was not advantageous. Some weapons such as the tessen (iron fan) were also popular with commoners forbidden by law from openly carrying bladed weapons.

As my research of these unusual weapons increased, I began writing articles about the subject for various martial arts magazines. Mr. George Donahue, then editor for Tuttle Publishing, offered invaluable advice and I self-published my first book, *Secret Weapons of Jujutsu*. Tuttle Publishing eventually purchased the rights and released a paperback edition.

After the first book was published, I received numerous questions, comments, and even additional tidbits of information from hundreds of martial arts practitioners, historical re-enactors, jidai-geki fans, and Japanese sword and armor collectors. I was quite fortunate to make the acquaintance of Nawa Yumio sensei, author of numerous titles about feudal-era arresting implements and procedures. Nawa sensei was also the last head of Masaki-ryū Manrikigusari-jutsu and Edo Machikata Jutte-jutsu as well as a technical consultant for many jidai-geki television shows and movies. Our visits and correspondence provided me with a wealth of information and details unavailable from any other source. Dr. S. Alexander Takeuchi, Department of Sociology at the University of North Alabama, provided considerable information regarding both feudal-era weapons restrictions and Edo-period publications. I also had the opportunity to conduct more in-depth research through visits to the Tokyo National Museum, Meiji University Criminology Museum, Keisatsu Museum, and Fukagawa Edo Museum. With the assistance and editorial guidance of Ms. Ashley Benning, editor for Tuttle Publishing, I wrote my second book, *Taiho-Jutsu: Law and Order in the Age of the Samurai*. A talented artist, good friend, and fellow judoka, Mr. Rich Hashimoto, provided excellent line drawings to illustrate many of the techniques.

After several years, I considered preparing a revised edition of *Secret Weapons of Jujutsu*. Instead, Ms. Sandra Korinchak, senior editor for Tuttle Publishing, suggested creating an entirely separate book with both updated and new material. With her advice and guidance, this is the result. Many individuals contributed information, assistance, and encouragement for this project. Without their help, this book would not have been realized. I am especially grateful to Ms. Korinchak for her editorial insights and her enthusiasm for this project. I also want to thank Mr. Hashimoto for allowing me to use several of his line drawings again for this volume. Finally, I want to thank my wife Lynn for her patience and understanding about my obsession with Japanese martial arts and history. Any errors are mine alone.

Japanese Martial Arts Culture

The samurai were Japan's warrior class for more than seven centuries. The word comes from the Japanese verb *saburau*, meaning "service to a noble." Samurai were primarily military retainers who attended and guarded clan leaders. The samurai eventually emerged as military aristocrats and then as military rulers. The samurai were also known as *bushi*, or "warriors."

Medieval samurai were generally illiterate, rural landowners who farmed between battles. With an economy based almost solely on agriculture, small farming villages were the core of early Japanese society. Area landowners and farmers also served as militia forces, either in the defense of their own lands or as private armies seeking to expand and gain new territories. As hereditary warriors, though, they were governed by a code of ethics—*bushidō*, meaning the "way of the warrior"—that defined service and conduct appropriate to their status as elite members of Japanese society. Even though the samurai's role changed from farmers and soldiers to government bureaucrats and administrators during the latter years of relative peace, the samurai were still bound by the tenets of bushidō and their warrior heritage.

Japan was theoretically ruled by the emperor, considered a direct descendant of the Sun Goddess Amaterasu Omikami. An extensive hereditary aristocracy of nobles formed the Imperial

Court, although the emperor and his nobles have held no real governing power for many centuries. Their position was mostly symbolic. Their principal function was to conduct and take part in various religious rituals.

An abbreviation of *seitaishōgun*, the title of shōgun first appeared during the Nara period (710–794) and means "great general to conquer barbarians." Initially a temporary designation, the shōgun were authorized to recruit soldiers to subdue the Ainu, an ethnic tribal group indigenous to the northern islands of Japan. Later the title of shōgun came to designate a supreme chief of samurai. During the Kamakura period (1185–1333), the title became permanent and was used until the late nineteenth century.

The shōgunate was first referred to as *bakufu*, a Chinese term designating the headquarters of a general in expedition. The term literally means "office under tent." After Minamoto no Yoritomo became shōgun and officially established the Kamakura bakufu, virtually replacing the prerogative of the Imperial Court, though, the term shōgunate was used to designate the military government. There were three successive shōgunate or military governments in Japan—Kamakura shōgunate (1185–1333), Muromachi shōgunate (1336–1573), and Edo shōgunate (1603–1868)—each designating the periods administered by the respective shōgun.

A dispute over shōgunal succession combined with harsh economic times eventually led to the *Onin no ran* (Onin war) in 1467, embroiling Japan in more than one hundred years of successive military disputes referred to as the Sengoku period. Many battles were fought constantly throughout Japan during this era, also referred to as the Warring States period. The introduction of guns to Japan by the Portuguese in 1543 served to intensify battlefield tactics and conflicts over territory.

A brilliant military strategist and son of a warlord, Oda Nobunaga (1534–1582) conquered most of Japan and declared shōgun in 1568 after entering the capital city of Kyōto. When Nobunaga was assassinated by Akechi Mitsuhide in 1582, one of his generals, Toyotomi Hideyoshi, avenged the murder and eventually unified Japan. Despite uncommon military and political talents, Hideyoshi was unable to assume the title of shōgun because of his family's modest background.

Tokugawa Ieyasu (1542–1616) was born into the family of a local warlord in the west of Aichi Prefecture. Located between two powerful clans, Imagawa in the east and Oda in the west, Ieyasu spent his youth as a hostage of those respective families. Ieyasu changed his name from Matsudaira to Tokugawa in 1566 although the sub-branches of the family were always called Matsudaira. After the death of Hideyoshi in 1598, Ieyasu established himself as Japan's shōgun after the decisive defeat of Ishida Mitsunari in the Battle at Sekigahara in 1600. For nearly three centuries (approximately 1603 to 1868), Japan existed as a feudal society under a relatively tranquil rule of the Tokugawa shōgunate. This Edo-based shōgunate lasted two hundred sixty-five years and is officially referred to as the Edo period.

During the Edo period, Japan was divided into roughly three hundred regional domains, inheritable lands or revenue-producing properties, called *han*. All but a few of the smaller han were governed by a *daimyō* (feudal lord) who swore loyalty to the Tokugawa shōgunate. Although the Tokugawa shōgunate closely monitored the military activities of each han, the daimyō were granted independence in their other domestic and economic policies. The daimyō held total power over their individual domains, answering only to the shōgunate. Each daimyō was also given complete power and authority to administer operations within his own han. This right often extended to jurisdiction over the samurai of the han even when serving outside their respective territories.

Among the daimyō, there were various ranks, mostly related to whether their clan had directly supported Ieyasu and his forces during the Battle at Sekigahara. Within each domain, the individual daimyō ruled over a varying number of direct retainers, which often included a very complicated hierarchy within their own samurai ranks resulting in various status levels. The Tokugawa clan's own direct retainers, called *hatamoto* or literally "banner men," also held many significant positions within the shōgunate, many equal in rank to the daimyō.

One method the Tokugawa shōgunate used to control the various daimyō was to impose heavy financial burdens through taxation and other means. Unable to support the high cost of a strong military, the daimyō were no longer able to wage clan wars with their severely reduced armies. Since there was often no more need for their military skills during this time of peace and the daimyō faced mounting expenses, the samurai as a class were transformed into military bureaucrats and required to master administrative skills as well as military arts. Some developed the necessary skills for bureaucratic service, but others did not.

Whether due their inability to master other skills or the abolishment of their respective han, many samurai were forced to become unemployed wanderers known as *rōnin*, a term literally meaning "wave man." Without a daimyō to serve and no steady source of income, they were generally at the mercy of circumstances, like men tossed about by waves in the ocean.

From the turn of the eighteenth century, the Japanese economy surged. For the first time, Japanese merchants became wealthy and powerful, despite their lower-class status in Japanese society. In the new affluent bourgeois culture, poor samurai frequently turned to opening *bujutsu* (military arts) schools as a way of making a living. Eventually many of these samurai began teaching their martial art skills to the more prosperous *chōnin* (townsmen).

As the Japanese economy evolved, there was also a great increase in criminal activities. Criminal elements such as the *yakuza*, or underworld gangs, first appeared during the Edo period in the Kanto area, where farmers found other employment due to the development of money-based economy. The yakuza became progressively more powerful and widespread during this period. Thus unarmed fighting techniques often proved to be quite popular with the townsmen, who were banned from carrying weapons other than short swords or knives due to their social status. Many townsmen and farmers also studied swordsmanship in the hope of distinguishing themselves and being raised to samurai status.

After the 1868 revolution in Japan, the Tokugawa shōgunate was overthrown and a constitutional monarchy, such as in England, was born. Many professional martial arts instructors who had served the shōgun and the many feudal lords by teaching their warriors suddenly lost their positions. Since samurai were now also prohibited from openly carrying swords, unarmed fighting skills were now often the only available means of self-defense or protection.

The Soul of the Samurai

The Japanese sword, admired for its artistic value as well as for its practical merits, is often considered an emblem of the samurai's power and skill. It was venerated by the bushi, or "warrior class," and the *daishō*, or set of two swords, was worn as a badge of a samurai's status. *Daishō* literally translates as "big-little" and refers to a pair of swords, consisting of one *daitō* (long sword) and a *shōtō* (short sword). Either sword was referred to as *katana*, although the short sword was sometimes called *wakizashi*. The sword was "the soul of a samurai," and no self-respecting bushi would be seen outside his home without his daishō prominently displayed.

During wartime, swordsmanship was essential for survival on the battlefield. However, the possession of suitable side arms was considered a samurai's responsibility even after the end of the Warring States period. As bureaucrats, the samurai had little actual need for arms, yet they were required to wear the daishō as a symbol of their status and their place in society. Under the Tokugawa shōgunate, extensive martial arts training and individual expertise with weapons declined significantly within the samurai class in general as their responsibilities shifted toward administration and management.

Despite popular literature and the images portrayed in samurai films, bushidō—the warrior's code of ethics and the samurai's moral precepts—did not allow for indiscriminate use of the sword. As bushidō stressed the proper use of the sword, it also detested its misuse. The samurai who drew his sword for unjustifiable reasons or at improper occasions was regarded as ill-mannered and crude.

Japanese swordsmiths would fast and undergo ritual purification before making a new blade. While working at their anvils, they wore white robes like Shinto priests. By the thirteenth century, Japanese swords were recognized as far superior to those made anywhere else in the world. No one could challenge the quality of the steel forged by these Japanese swordsmiths.

To hold a sharp edge, steel needed to be hard. However, hard steel is also brittle and could break in battle. Soft steel was more flexible and wouldn't break as easily, but soft steel would not hold a sharp edge, quickly dulling through use. The Japanese swordsmiths solved this problem by hammering layers of steel of varying hardness together. Then they reheated the metal layers, folded the metal back on itself, and hammered it out thin again and again. After a dozen times, the steel consisted of thousands of paper-thin laminations of hard and soft metal. When it was ground to a sharp edge, the hard metal stood out and resisted dulling, while the soft steel kept the sword from breaking.

Finally, the master swordsmith covered the roughly finished blade with a thick layer of clay, leaving the edge exposed. The blade was then heated until the glowing metal reached the proper shade of color, then it was quickly submerged into cool water. The exposed edge cooled instantly while the rest of the blade, protected by the clay, cooled slowly and remained comparatively soft.

The final result was a flexible sword blade of soft non-brittle metal enclosed in a thin layer of hard steel. The edge, though, consisted of tempered hardened steel which would hold its razor sharpness despite repeated use.

The development of the samurai sword is based in Japanese mythology. According to legend, the Sun Goddess Amaterasu Omikami gave the first sword to her grandson, Ninigi-no Mikoto, to use as he ruled over Japan. The early warriors thought their swords had astonishing power and even their own individual personalities. There are many stories about the spiritual powers and sharpness of exceptional blades. One legend is about the products of two famous swordsmiths, Muramasa and Masume. Two warlords, who each owned a different craftsman's sword, often argued about which one of the swordsmiths was the most skilled. Finally they decided on a test.

The first held his blade, an excellent katana made by Muramasa, in a swift running stream. A dead leaf drifted against the edge of the sword and was cut cleanly in half. The other put his sword made by Masume in the stream. Instead of being cut, though, the floating leaves passed on either side. They decided that the second blade was superior because the maker had endowed his blade with a spirit which caused the leaves to avoid its edge.

This legend speaks volumes in explaining the true nature of Japanese morals and ethics. The skill to create a blade so sharp that it was capable of cutting through even a leaf floating in the stream was obviously highly regarded. However, the blade endowed with a spirit to avoid cutting when unnecessary was even more valued.

It is clear that the Japanese admired those who avoided the use of the sword if other means were available to resolve their problems. Admiration for the spiritual and moral values of humanity and compassion despite the harsh times and lifestyles are found in many of the stories and records concerning everyday Japanese life during the feudal period.

There are many other reasons a feudal era samurai might be reluctant to use his sword. Many of the Japanese swords were family heirlooms, passed down from generation to generation. Even a basic katana represented a major investment for samurai of any class. As such, it would have been unwise to draw and risk damaging such an expensive blade just to settle a minor altercation.

It was not uncommon for many samurai to firmly tie the *tsuba* (handguard) of their sword to the *saya* (scabbard). They would frequently use a twisted piece of paper or thin twine for this purpose. The reason was to prevent the sword from inadvertently falling from the scabbard and possibly being damaged. Obviously, this also prevented them from rapidly drawing the sword as well. As a badge of samurai class, the daishō was important for samurai to wear in public to identify themselves. During an extended period of peace such as the Edo period, though, it is apparent that many samurai had no intention of using their swords in haste.

Unarmed Fighting

Various techniques of unarmed fighting have developed in almost all cultures, but these skills received special attention in Japan. The use of *jūjutsu*, or unarmed fighting techniques, can be traced back to Japan's mythological age. The Japanese gods Kashima and Kadori were said to have first used jūjutsu techniques to punish the lawless inhabitants of the eastern provinces.

Early traces of the Japanese appreciation for unarmed fighting traditions can also be found in written records. For example, documents dated nearly two thousand years ago record that Emperor Suinin ordered two men, Nomi-no-Sukune and Taima-no-Kuehaya, to a wrestling contest. After a lengthy match apparently consisting mainly of kicking, Nomi-no-Sukune gained the advantage over Taima-no-Kuehaya, knocking his opponent to the ground and trampling him to death.

During the Sengoku period, Japan was the scene of many lengthy civil wars and continuous strife. It was on these bloody and violent battlefields that the art of *kumiuchi*, a form of wrestling while both participants are wearing armor, originated and developed. Eventually, the art of kumiuchi advanced to the point that it was not unusual for a weaker opponent to gain victory over a stronger foe, thus encouraging many aspiring warriors to train themselves in this unique fighting style.

As the art of kumiuchi gained popularity, various schools of unarmed fighting sprang up in Japan. The various unarmed fighting styles were known by other names such as jūjutsu, taijutsu, yawara, wajutsu, toride, kogusoku, kempo, hakuda, shuhaku, jūdo, and many others, each slightly different applications of nearly identical principles. Although such schools focused on unarmed fighting techniques, many styles incorporated common everyday implements as improvised weapons or developed specialized weapons and trained in special skills for their use.

These styles quickly became so intermingled with each other that is virtually impossible to distinguish them from one another now. However, the purpose of toride and kogusoku was primarily to restrain and arrest persons, while the intent of jūjutsu and jūdo was to throw or kill one's opponent; and kempo and hakuda emphasized the use of kicks or strikes against opponents. In general, all of these styles may be described as unarmed fighting techniques for use against an armed or an unarmed opponent. Frequently the various styles might also include the use of common everyday implements or small specialized weapons to defeat an enemy armed with a larger weapon.

In most traditional Japanese fighting arts, training is centered on *kata*, or the repeated practice of fixed, formal training exercises. Each technique is performed by two persons acting in predefined roles and in carefully rendered steps. The person applying the offensive or defensive technique is commonly referred to as *tori*, while the person receiving the technique is called *uke*. Some styles use shitachi when tori is armed with a sword and shite when unarmed or armed with other weapons. Likewise, uke is often called *uchitachi* when armed with a sword, *uchite* when armed with other weapons, and *ukete* when unarmed.

Both tori and uke execute specific patterns or steps in a controlled, ritualized manner. Each kata includes vital elements for either offense or defense. However, the concept of kata is often misunderstood. Although various techniques are executed, kata should not be considered a catalog of designated responses to specific dangerous situations. Rather, kata is a method of transmitting core principles and tactics.

Each individual *ryūha*, or school, typically incorporated different movements, usually fixed in historical tradition and classical conventions, within its respective kata practice. The stylistic performance of these steps often varied between schools, with different forms for entering the kata and acknowledging each other, as well as for concluding techniques and finishing the kata. What remains is the essence of the technique, from initiation of an attack to the resolution whereby tori ultimately disarms and defeats uke, either by restraint or by more lethal methods.

Unarmed fighting styles branched into many different schools. Many have little if any reliable records, even regarding their founders, thus making it very difficult to identify the origins. Some accounts credit the development of unarmed fighting styles to techniques imported from China. Based on reliable records, though, other scholars believe that the development of unarmed fighting styles is indigenous to Japan and not based on foreign influences. That debate aside, the following are some descriptions of just a few of the more well-known schools which started during this period.

Takenouchi-ryū

Takenouchi-ryū was founded by Takenouchi Hisamori, a native of Haga village in the province of Mimasaka. During a period of meditation at Sannomiya Shrine in June 1532, he fell asleep after an intensive solitary training session. According to the tradition, a yamabushi, a member of a religious class which frequently traveled throughout Japan, appeared and taught several techniques for disarming and restraining opponents to Takenouchi. The yamabushi also convinced him of the advantages of small arms over larger weapons. Takenouchi named this style kogusoku, and the art still exists today after many generations of successors.

Kito-ryū

Kito-ryū was founded by Terada Kanyemon, a retainer of Kyogoku Tango-no-Kami. He first learned unarmed fighting skills from Terada Heizayemon, who was a teacher of Fukuno-ryu, a school originated by Fukuno Shichiroyemon. (Fukuno Shichiroyemon, along with Miura Yojiyemon and Isogai Jirozayemon, initially studied kempo under Chin Gempin, a Chinese who traveled to Kokushoji Temple at Azabu in Edo during the latter part of the seventeenth century. The three rōnin each founded their own jūjutsu schools.) After mastering jūjutsu skills, Terada Kanyemon founded his own school which he called Kito-ryū. Throwing skills are very prominent in this style, a characteristic especially noted in the stylized forms used to teach and demonstrate the techniques of Kito-ryū.

Shibukawa-ryū

The founder of Shibukawa-ryū, Shibukawa Bangoro trained in unarmed fighting skills under Sekiguchi Hachirozaemon, the son of Sekiguchi Jushin. After developing great proficiency, he opened his own school in Edo. During the peace of the Edo period, Shibukawa-ryū was noted for developing the arts of tessen-jutsu and jutte-jutsu. (See Chapter Four for more information on tessen-jutsu and Chapter Five for more information about jutte-jutsu.)

Yoshin-ryū

There are two different accounts of the Yoshin-ryū source. The first states the founder as Miura Yoshin, a physician in Nagasaki. Convinced that physical illness was the result of an imbalance between the use of mind and body, he developed a number of techniques for disarming and restraining an opponent by utilizing his principles for resolving this imbalance. After his death, two of his first followers established their own schools, respectively called Miura-ryū and Yoshin-ryū after the family and given names of the originator.

A second account claims Akiyama Shirobei Yoshitoki, also a physician from Nagasaki, to be the founder. While studying medicine in China, he also learned several *te,* or "fighting tricks," as well as many different *kappo* (resuscitation techniques). Upon his return to Japan, Akiyama began teaching his fighting style, but was dissatisfied with the limited number of techniques. Determined to improve his fighting proficiency and develop a wider range of techniques, he retired to the Temmangu temple at Tsukushi for several months to meditate and seek inspiration.

It was a harsh winter, and Akiyama watched as the snow fell on the temple grounds. He noticed the sturdy branches of the surrounding trees often broke and were crushed under the weight of accumulated snow. However, the weaker willow-tree was able to escape this fate due to the suppleness of its branches. The flexible branches bent and gave way as the weight increased, thus allowing them to throw off the snow and spring back after releasing their burden. Akiyama was so impressed, he based his new fighting techniques on this concept, giving his sect the name Yoshin-ryū, which means "willow-heart school."

Kushin-ryū

Kushin-ryū was founded by Inouye Nagakatsu. However, his grandson, Inouye Nagayasu (generally known as Gumbei), was so adept in jūjutsu that he is often credited as being the originator. This style closely resembles the Kito-ryū style, especially in the emphasis on throwing skills. It is stated that Inouye Nagayasu trained for some time under Takino, a former student of Kito-ryū.

Tenjin-shinyo-ryū

Tenjin-shinyo-ryū was founded by Iso Matayemon, a retainer of the Kii clan. A native of the Matsuzaka in Ise province, he studied under Hitosuyanagi Oribe, a master of Yoshin-ryū. Following the death of his teacher, he later studied under Homma Joyemon, an adept in Shin-no-Shinto-ryū. Convinced from his actual fighting experiences that victory required the skillful application of *atemi*, the art of striking the vital and vulnerable points of an opponent's body, Iso Matayemon emphasized atemi in the founding of his own style. He called his new style Tenjin-shinyo-ryū, deriving the name partially from both Yoshin-ryū and Shin-no-Shinto-ryū.

Shintō Musō-ryū

Although primarily concerned with the arts of the sword and staff, Shintō Musō-ryū has also incorporated many other auxiliary arts since its inception. Shintō Musō-ryū was founded by Muso Gonnosuke Katsuyoshi during the early part of the Edo period. The third successor of the Shintō Musō-ryū, Matsuzaki Kinueumon Tsunekatsu added Ittatsu-ryū hojo-jutsu (rope binding) from Ittatsu-ryū, and jutte-jutsu (truncheon art) from Ikkaku-ryū, to the Shintō Musō-ryū curriculum.

In more recent years, the Japanese police modified many of the same Ikkaku-ryū jutte-jutsu techniques from the Shintō Musō-ryū curriculum for their *keisatsu keibo-jutsu* (police baton art) training. Although the basic techniques are similar, the targets and applications of keisatsu keibo-jutsu techniques have been modified slightly to enable police officers to more effectively control a suspect with minimum injury, rather than to put the individual down at any cost.

Disarming the Populace

Prior to the end of the Sengoku period, most able-bodied subjects were armed with various weapons to some degree. As Japan became unified, though, a heavily armed populace was considered a significant threat to the new government. To discourage uprisings and revolt, Hideyoshi Toyotomi initiated a series of legislative social reforms. These edicts strictly defined social classes and drastically restricted social mobility.

In 1588 Hideyoshi issued the *Taiko no katanagari* (sword hunt), a decree prohibiting the possession of swords and guns by all but the noble classes. Claiming that the possession of weapons by peasants "makes difficult the collection of taxes and tends to foment uprisings," the mandate prohibited farmers from possessing long or short swords, bows, spears, muskets, or any other form of weapon. Local daimyō, official agents, and deputies were ordered to collect all such weapons within their jurisdictions and deliver them to be melted down to supply materials for construction of a temple containing a massive Buddha.

The proposal for creating a Buddhist image from destroyed weapons was meant to placate pious warrior monks as well as religiously devout commoners. This edict also met with widespread daimyō approval. Local rulers realized that disarming peasants also effectively restricted their neighbors from quickly raising a militia should any potential territorial disputes arise. Once the weapons were collected, though, Hideyoshi ordered them melted down and used to build a statue in his own likeness.

As a result of the sword hunt edict, only members of the warrior class were permitted to wear the daishō, thus differentiating samurai from the rest of the population. Three years later, Hideyoshi issued another edict clearly segregating the population into four major social castes—warrior, farmer, craftsman, and merchant. It further isolated and restricted interaction between different classes and denied any changes in social status.

Below the samurai or bushi class were the *nōmin* (farmers). The nōmin were considered second in class only to the samurai because they provided the crops and livestock necessary to feed the population. The creation of mutually exclusive farming and military social castes was calculated to prevent formation of alliances. Although they represented by far the largest segment of the population, the unarmed nōmin were weak and relatively helpless against military forces. And while the samurai were armed and trained in battlefield tactics, their overall numbers were comparatively small, representing less than one-tenth of the total populace at any one time. Yet Hideyoshi recognized the potential threat facing the new administration should nōmin and samurai join forces for revolution. To prevent this, the samurai were forced to move away from their villages and farms and to live within garrison towns.

The next lower classes lived in towns and were called *chōnin* (townsmen). These craftsmen and artisans formed the third tier of the feudal Japanese caste system. They were held in nominal favor since they produced the tools and utensils needed by the farmers and the weapons and associated decorations required by the bushi.

The fourth tier consisted of merchants, who were looked down upon because they essentially created nothing while basically living off the produce of others. Although they were considered fairly low in the social structure, the merchant class owned most of the actual property by the nineteenth century. Many became bankers, not only financing other merchant ventures, but also lending money to the members of the samurai class. As the richest members of the society, they frequently bought titles or married into samurai families to improve their status.

Members of the samurai class had for many years considered financial issues as beneath their dignity and even disdained the handling of money. This extended to having their servants actually pay for all necessities to avoid contact with coins. Physically touching money was considered unclean, and most samurai would wrap their coins in paper before presenting them for payment to another.

As a result, many samurai were not very adept at dealing with fiscal issues and so now often found themselves in serious financial straits. Ironically, many of their rights and power, including the carrying of weapons, were often circumscribed by the bankers and money lenders from the merchant class.

The lowest class consisted of the *hinan* (outcasts) or *eta* who were basically considered to be non-humans. The term *eta* literally means "filth," and the eta were ostracized by the rest of Edo period society. The eta often performed the tasks believed to be spiritually unclean, such as dealing with the dead. For example, they often worked in trades associated with tanning leather or disposing of animal and human carcasses. As a result, eta were the target of tremendous social prejudices. Even within this group existed a varied ranking system, from those who were temporarily classed as outcasts due to their circumstances, such as convicted petty criminals, to those who were hereditary and permanent pariahs in the rigid feudal Japanese social order.

In the last of his social reform efforts, Hideyoshi commissioned a land census, establishing a uniform tax system and further restricting physical movement between the various provinces, or han, under his rule. Each individual was required to register his name, along with his status and his number of houses. All registered individuals were then prohibited from moving to any other province, or han, without prior government approval.

Following the death of Hideyoshi and the establishment of the Tokugawa shōgunate in 1603, these social policies were further enforced with even more government proclamations. Barrier stations, or *seki*, were established on all major highways, and travelers were searched for any contraband or defiance of rules regarding physical movement. The Tokugawa shōgunate was known for the policy to prevent *Irideppo ni deonna* (incoming firearms and fleeing women), which prohibited transport of arms and restricted women, especially daimyō family members held as potential hostages, from leaving the city.

Although samurai openly carried razor-sharp swords, chōnin and nōmin during the Edo period usually were not allowed such overt displays of weaponry. Restricted by government decrees, they often resorted to *hibuki* (hidden or concealed weapons) for personal protection.

While katana were prohibited, chōnin and nōmin were still allowed to carry *tantō* (daggers) as well as short swords known as wakizashi. Commoners did not always abide by the laws prohibiting swords. One reason was that the actual measurements used to define katana, wakizashi, and tantō were confusing and often inconsistently applied in many of these laws. Thus during the early part of the Edo period (early 1600s), some chōnin, and especially yakuza, or criminal gang members, openly carried long wakizashi that were virtually equivalent to prohibited katana.

The Japanese historic measure of length, called the *kanejaku* (square), originated in China and is a common measurement system used for centuries in countries surrounding the Sea of Japan and the East China Sea. Designated Japan's official measure in 701 by the Taiho Code, the length is made up of units called bu, sun, shaku, and ken. One bu is equal to 0.1193 inches (0.303 centimeters). Ten bu equal one sun, or 1.193 inches (3.03 centimeters). Ten sun equal one shaku, or 11.93 inches (30.3 centimeters). And six shaku equal one ken, or 71.58 inches (181.8 centimeters).

In an effort to restore peace and order to their society, the Tokugawa shōgunate issued various orders prohibiting chōnin from carrying long swords. One such government order was the *Daishō katana no sumpō oyobi touhatsu futsumō no sei* (the order regarding daishō katana and hair style), issued in July 1645. This law specified the maximum blade length of katana as 2 shaku 8 or 9 sun, or roughly 34 inches (86 centimeters). The blade length of wakizashi was restricted to 1 shaku 8 or 9 sun or about 22 inches (56 centimeters).

In March 1668, the Tokugawa shōgunate once again issued *Mutō rei* (no sword order), an executive directive firmly prohibiting the chōnin class from carrying any swords longer than *ko-wakizashi*, a very short sword, without specific government permission. According to the edict, the ko-wakizashi blade length was defined as being no longer than 1 shaku 5 sun or approximately 17 inches (45 centimeters). The feudal government later revised this executive order, adding some specific exceptions to this prohibition, including the right for chōnin to carry regular-length wakizashi when traveling or during fires.

Commoners were allowed to carry a wakizashi on trips to protect themselves and their valuables from brigands who often preyed on travelers. Since fires in the densely populated city of Edo occurred with such frequency, most chōnin would take their household possessions into the streets with them when evacuating their neighborhood. The government decree thus allowed them to arm themselves and protect their personal possessions during such chaotic events.

Although not specifically prohibited from carrying ko-wakizashi, law-abiding chōnin during the Edo period typically did not wear any swords while conducting their day-to-day business within the city. Because of the risks of encountering bandits or worse, though, it was quite common for chōnin to openly wear a legal-length ko-wakizashi when traveling any significant distance from their homes.

Kirisutegomen

Popular fiction has often portrayed the samurai as extremely violent and quick to cut someone down at the slightest provocation. With a rigidly enforced and unquestioned social hierarchy, some samurai did tend to be rather dismissive, even arrogant and abusive toward the lower classes. It is a popular misconception, though, that most samurai swaggered about the streets of Edo or rural highways indiscriminately killing one another or some unfortunate chōnin and nōmin out of anger over the slightest perceived offense. Although this type of incident is a widespread occurrence in historical dramas and novels, the truth is actually much more mundane.

It is true that the convention of *kirisutegomen* ("killing and going away") was formally recognized under the Tokugawa shōgunate. According to this custom, samurai basically had the legally recognized right to kill any member of the common classes acting other than as expected. Unexpected behavior included surliness, discourtesy, and inappropriate conduct. This occasionally fostered the practice of *tsuji-giri*, testing a sword blade by cutting down a commoner.

Any samurai involved in such a killing, however, would certainly have been held by officials while an investigation was conducted. The Tokugawa shōgunate published a series of guidelines, such as the *Kujikata osadamegaki*, that established strict penal codes and judicial procedures. Any samurai found guilty of inappropriate behavior was often subjected to severe penalties. The *metsuke* (watchers) served as the overseers and inspectors for retainers in the service of the various daimyō. Unemployed samurai or rōnin were considered under the jurisdiction of the respective *machi-bugyō* (town magistrate), though, and subject to many of the same penal codes as any chōnin.

Wasteful actions such as kirisutegomen, and especially tsuji-giri, were generally frowned upon by all clan and government officials. Although it may have been allowed legally, such behavior was definitely considered intolerable according to commonly accepted religious, moral, and ethical values. The government, realizing it was dependent upon the common people for both produce and taxes, would not risk further alienation by allowing such excesses. Even if an investigation did fail to find any infraction of these guidelines, no samurai could afford a reputation for such needless killings.

According to common law of this period, any citizen, regardless of class, was also allowed to defend himself from unprovoked attacks. Thus, a commoner was allowed to kill a samurai if assaulted. If successful, he was likely to be released from any murder charges by authorities if the killing was committed in self-defense. Obviously, samurai were not as prone to indulge in practices such as kirisute-gomen and tsuji-giri when commoners were armed and capable of offering resistance.

Fukushū and Ada-uchi

Killing another samurai, even a lower-ranking bushi, might easily spark a *fukushū* (blood feud) with another clan, resulting in many other members of either house being killed. No self-respecting bushi would dare put his fellow clan members in such a dangerous position without considering these possible consequences.

Slaying any individual, regardless of class, might also initiate an *ada-uchi*, a legal vendetta, by members of the victim's family. (The colloquial term *kataki-uchi* is a less formal, common reference for such a quarrel.) According to the strict rules of ada-uchi, retaliation could be directed only against the murderer and then only by a person of equal or lower social status. An ada-uchi required registration with local officials. Once a permit was issued, the right or wrong of the original death was considered irrelevant. Anyone killing another without a properly registered ada-uchi, though, was subject to punishment for murder.

Yamamoto Tsunetomo (1658–1719), a Buddhist priest and former retainer of Nabeshima Mitsushige, third daimyō of Saga, shared a series of anecdotes over several years with Tashiro Tsuramoto, a samurai from the Nabeshima fief in Kyushu. Recorded by the younger samurai and published as *Hagakure* [Hidden Leaves], these offer many insights into daily life and attitudes of his era. The following example illustrates how a samurai might be expected to commit *seppuku* (ritual suicide) to atone for brawling and murder:

A certain son of Mori Monbei got into a fight and returned home wounded. Asked by Monbei, "What did you do to your opponent?" his son replied, "I cut him down."

When Monbei asked, "Did you deliver the coup de grace?" his son replied, "Indeed I did." [This coup de grace was called todome *and typically consisted of stabbing the wounded man through the neck.]*

Then Monbei said, "You have certainly done well, and there is nothing to regret. Now, even if you fled you would have to commit seppuku anyway. When your mood improves, commit seppuku, and rather than die by another's hand, you can die by your father's." And soon after he performed kaishaku for his son. [The kaishaku serves as a second during seppuku. After the initial incisions are made in the abdomen, the kaishaku is expected to decapitate the subject with one swift sword stroke, thus sparing him from further suffering.]

The Forty-seven Rōnin Incident

It was such an impetuous and foolhardy act that resulted in one of the most famous of Japanese legends. The Forty-seven Rōnin incident is a story reflecting many of the ideals of Japan's samurai. In 1701, Lord Asano Nagamori, a brash young daimyō from Ako, was ordered to commit seppuku and his clan was abolished, thus setting the stage for the bloodiest vendetta in Japan's history. Asano's offense was drawing his short sword and attacking the shōgun's chief of protocol, Kira Yoshinaka, during preparations for an official reception of an imperial envoy from Kyōto.

Various reasons are given for the shōgun's harsh sentencing of Lord Asano. Most historians agree that it was for drawing his short sword and wounding Yoshinaka, although one account also records that after the initial attack failed, Lord Asano threw his wakizashi at the chief of protocol, damaging a lacquered screen. Ultimately, though, it was Lord Asano's obvious disregard for prohibitions against drawing one's sword within the palace grounds that sealed his fate.

The shōgun's failure to have Kira share in the responsibility angered Asano's retainers, who felt that Kira's improper actions were ignored and Asano's punishment was too harsh. When a daimyō committed seppuku, his castle was confiscated by the shōgun, his family disinherited, and his samurai retainers ordered to disband, thus becoming rōnin. Oishi Kuranosuke, Asano's chief councilor, had a plan, though, to avenge Asano's disgrace by killing Kira, who had brought their clan to such a tragic end.

The men split up to conceal their plans from Kira, who naturally suspected that Asano's retainers would seek revenge. Oishi went to Yamashina, a suburb of Kyoto, where he earned a reputation as a drunken gambler, a ruse that successfully deceived the shōgun's many spies. For nearly two years, the rōnin waited, disguised as merchants, street vendors, and even drunks. When suspicions were finally relaxed, Oishi and the other rōnin decided that their time had come. One by one, Oishi and his men infiltrated Edo, and on the snowy winter night of December 14, 1702, the Forty-seven Rōnin attacked Kira's mansion while he was hosting a tea party.

After killing Kira, the rōnin took his head to Asano's grave at Sengaku-ji temple. For their actions, the shōgun ordered the rōnin to commit seppuku. After their deaths, the Forty-seven Rōnin were buried next to their master at Sengaku-ji temple. Today, the Forty-seven Rōnin are memorialized in a play called *Chusingura* which celebrates the theme of their sacrifice in the name of loyalty. Each year thousands of Japanese visit the gravesites at Sengaku-ji temple to pay homage to the honor and loyalty of the Forty-seven Rōnin and their dedication to the code of bushidō. Although their loyalty has become legendary, the fact remains that the Asano family and their clan were destroyed by Lord Asano's one moment of rage and his inopportune use of his sword.

2

Improvised Weapons

One of the Edo period's most famous samurai, Yagyū Jūbei Mitsuyoshi would probably have been relegated to obscurity in Japanese history if modern storytellers were not intrigued by a lapse of twelve years from his life in official records.

A minor daimyō family, the Yagyū held lands in present day Nara Prefecture and founded the Yagyū Shinkage-ryū style of martial arts. Following a superb display of swordsmanship by Yagyū Muneyoshi and his younger son, Tajima no Kami Munenori, in 1594 in Kyoto, Tokugawa Ieyasu employed Munenori as kenjutsu instructor for the Tokugawa clan. Munenori fought on the side of the Tokugawa during the battle of Sekigahara, after which his pupil became the first Tokugawa shōgun (Japan's military government leader). Yagyū Munenori continued to serve as official kenjutsu instructor to the Tokugawa shōgunate in Edo for three generations, passing the position to his son, Yagyū Jūbei Mitsuyoshi.

Not much is actually known about Yagyū Jūbei Mitsuyoshi. Born Shichiro, he grew up in the Yagyū family's domain near Nara until moving to Edo in 1616 to become an attendant to the second Tokugawa shōgun, Tokugawa Hidetada. Eventually he assumed his father's role as kenjutsu instructor under the third Tokugawa shōgun, Tokugawa Iemitsu. Although generally regarded as the best skilled swordsman in the Yagyū Shinkage-ryū, the 24-year-old

Jūbei was summarily dismissed by the shōgun, supposedly for drunkenness. He is not heard from again in the records until 1643 when a 36-year-old Jūbei suddenly reappears at a martial arts demonstration before the shōgun, after which he is inexplicably reinstated as kenjutsu instructor to the Tokugawa shōgunate.

It was a common Japanese practice to embark on long pilgrimages to religiously significant temples and shrines to obtain spiritual enlightenment through physical effort. To supplement and enhance their martial arts training, Japanese samurai would occasionally wander throughout the countryside, supposedly to challenge other schools and to further develop their own skills by matching themselves against worthy opponents. This form of spiritual and physical training is referred to as *musha-shugyō* (warrior journey).

The missing twelve years and the lack of specific evidence has led many to speculate that his dismissal was actually a scheme devised to allow Yagyū Jūbei Mitsuyoshi to travel through various provinces on a musha-shugyō while secretly collecting information on political and military activities for the Tokugawa shōgunate. The mystery surrounding his whereabouts during this period has also sparked various myths and legends. One of the best known is the legend of Yagyū Matajuro, a story illustrating the importance of the mental state known in Zen Buddhism as *zanshin* (constant peripheral awareness).

According to the legend, Matajuro grew up learning the forms of Yagyū Shinkage-ryū. Disappointed by his son's lazy nature and general lack of talent, however, Matajuro's father banished him from training in the family tradition. Deeply hurt by his father's abrupt dismissal, Matajuro resolved to learn kenjutsu from a master teacher and return someday as a great swordsman. Hearing stories of a swordsman with remarkable skills, Matajuro traveled to the han of Kii where he found a hermit named Banzo living in the mountains near the Kumano shrine.

Treated much like apprentices serving under master craftsmen, martial arts students residing within their instructor's home and training hall were generally referred to as *uchi-deshi* (inside student). Banzo accepted Matajuro as his uchi-deshi, and Matajuro moved into Banzo's simple hut, assuming responsibility for many of the domestic tasks. After several months of performing physical chores without receiving any lessons in the martial arts, though, a frustrated Matajuro finally demanded that Banzo teach him kenjutsu skills. Later that afternoon as Matajuro chopped wood, Banzo snuck up and struck Matajuro from behind with a wooden sword. Ashamed by his apparent inability to avoid the old man's sudden and unexpected attack, Matajuro resolved to concentrate harder and to remain on guard against further assaults.

For the next several months and with increasing frequency, Banzo would strike at Matjuro with the wooden sword at various times, whenever he believed his student was distracted or inattentive. Constantly guarding himself from these repeated attacks, Matajuro found his senses became heightened and he was eventually able to avoid more and more of his teacher's strikes. One evening as Matajuro was cooking rice over a fire, Banzo attacked him again by surprise. Wthout taking his mind off stirring the rice, Matajuro grabbed the wooden pot lid and fended off the blow. That same night, Banzo presented Manjuro with a certificate of mastery.

The legend stresses the importance of remaining constantly aware of the environment and changing circumstances even when performing simple everyday tasks. In dangerous and unpredictable times, a person must be prepared to defend oneself from unexpected attacks with whatever is available. As discussed in the previous chapter, though, a sword was often considered unsuitable or might be unavailable for use in an unforeseen confrontation. For personal defense in unpredictable events, therefore, samurai and chōnin frequently relied on alternative implements as improvised weapons in such situations.

This included the creative use of whatever common, everyday objects could be found at hand. Such items were often referred to as

微
直
物

mijikimono

mijikimono, which literally translates as "small, readily available objects." The use of ordinary implements—whether it be rice cooking pot lids or more personal items such as tobacco pipes, portable writing sets, or even decorative hairpins—for self-defense purposes can be found in various feudal era accounts.

Unlike the thin colored belts worn by modern-day martial arts practitioners, Japanese men generally wore a very long and stiff obi around their waists. Typically, they wore sashes anywhere from 2 to 3 sun wide or about 2 to 3 inches (6 to 9 centimeters), and 10 shaku long or roughly 10 feet (3 meters). The man's betsuzome-kaku obi was usually made of a thick cloth material, double sewn and often with additional cotton material stitched inside. The obi was tied with a special knot called *kai-no-uchi* (shell mouth) because of its unique shape. The knot was placed to the back of the kimono, just off center to the right-hand side.

Figure 1. Most men carried any number of items tucked in their *obi*. In an emergency, these *mijikimono* could be easily used as a self-defense weapon for striking, thrusting, or even blocking their opponent's weapon.

Whether samurai, artisans, or merchants, men usually carried a variety of common everyday implements tucked into their obi. For example, they would usually carry some medicines in a special tiered case called an inrō. Other items might include a pipe case with a tobacco pipe and pouch, a case for holding a brush and some ink for writing, or even utensils such as a small knife and other implements for dining.

Held in the fist, though, many of these items could also be used for striking, thrusting, or even blocking an opponent's weapon. Like the yawara-bō used in many jūjutsu styles, these improvised fist loads could often be used for impromptu self-defense. Figure 1 shows a number of typical mijikimono that samurai and chōnin might carry tucked into their obi. These were sometimes referred to as *tenouchi*, which literally means something "inside the hand."

tenouchi

Kiseru

Many samurai and chōnin smoked tobacco during the Edo period, so it was not uncommon to carry a *kiseru* (tobacco pipe). These were usually carried in a special case called a *kiseruzutsu*, which were made of leather, wood, woven straw, bamboo, or animal horn. There was also often a small tobacco pouch called a *tobako-ire* made of leather or lacquered woven straw, connected to the kiseruzutsu by a thin hemp cord. The typical Japanese kiseru had a much smaller bowl than western-style smoking pipes. The middle section often consisted of a hollow tube of bamboo or some other type of wood with two metal ends made of iron, silver, or bronze. Because of the high cost of importing tobacco, smoking was considered an extravagance of the rich. Therefore, many skilled Edo period artisans created kiseru from precious metals and adorned them with elaborate artwork and intricate detail as status symbols for their owners. Figure 2 is a typical Edo period kiseru and case.

Figure 2. The typical Japanese *kiseru* consisted of a *rau* (stem) made of bamboo or some other type of hollow wooden tube, fitted at each end with a *suikuchi* (mouthpiece) and *gankubi* (bowl) usually both made of iron, silver, or bronze.

Whether for the rich or the poor, the length of a typical Japanese kiseru intended primarily as a personal smoking accessory varied between 6 to 10 sun or approximately 6 to 10 inches (18 to 30 centimeters). Basically hard rods with metal ends, these were suitable as an impromptu self-defense thrusting or stabbing weapon if needed for an emergency.

The yakuza, gamblers and gangsters that lived on the fringes of society, as well as the *otokodate* "young man" and *machi-yakko* "street fellow," self-styled guardians of the common people, often carried much heavier and longer than normal kiseru which were intentionally designed to be used as weapons. Made much thicker and stronger than an ordinary smoking pipe, these were called *kenka kiseru*, literally "fighting pipes," and were anywhere from 1 shaku to 1 shaku 8 sun long or approximately 12 to 18 inches (30 to 54 centimeters). The kenka kiseru were often made completely of cast iron or brass, although a few had stems of thick hardwood. As such, the kenka kiseru served as a very effective truncheon-like weapon for hitting or striking an opponent.

There are a few rare examples of kenka kiseru as long as 4 shaku (approximately 4 feet or 120 centimeters) and even including *tsuba* (handguards) much like the typical katana or wakizashi. These extra-long kenka kiseru could easily be used like a heavy staff or long club in defense against a sword-wielding opponent.

The samurai often carried an even larger and heavier tobacco pipe specifically designed as a weapon for those rare occasions when a samurai was parted from his swords and yet still required some means of self-protection. Referred to as *buyōkiseru*, these custom made pipe stems were typically made entirely of cast iron or brass. More elaborate than the common kiseru, the buyōkiseru often included silver mouthpieces and bowls. The typical buyōkiseru was about 1 shaku 6 sun long or roughly 16 inches (48 centimeters), and could be easily carried or worn tucked into the obi without arousing undue suspicion.

Because kiseru were so frequently employed as a weapon during the Edo period, a number of classical martial arts schools incorporated special secret techniques into their curriculum. The styles of fighting armed with a kiseru were even commonly referred to as kiseru-jutsu and were often quite similar to those used in tessen-jutsu. (See Chapter 4 for more detailed information regarding tessen-jutsu.)

Yatate

The *yatate* is a Japanese portable writing set developed during the Kamakura period (1185–1333). The Japanese traditional way of writing is with a *fude* (brush) and *sumi* (ink). Before writing, one had to make their own ink by grinding an ink stick with water on a *suzuri* (flat grinding stone). Developed many centuries ago, this method of writing with a brush is still used today.

Samurai commonly carried a small ink grinding stone in a drawer near the bottom of their arrow stand so they could write letters and reports from the battlefield. This grinding stone was known as the *yatate no suzuri* (arrow stand grinding stone) or more simply as yatate. Because it was tiresome to grind fresh ink before writing, a method of soaking a piece of cotton or silk with ink and letting it dry was eventually devised. The small piece of cloth drenched in ink could be easily carried without spillage. Simply pressing a brush moistened with water to the cloth provided sufficient ink for writing a few characters.

The first portable writing sets were made in the shape of a *hiogi-gata* (closed or folded fan). Both the ink-soaked cloth and writing brush were covered by a hinged lid. Like the grinding stones they replaced, these portable writing sets were carried by the samurai in their quivers along with their arrows, so these writing sets continued to be referred to as yatate. Figure 3 shows an early yatate made in the shape of a hiogi-gata.

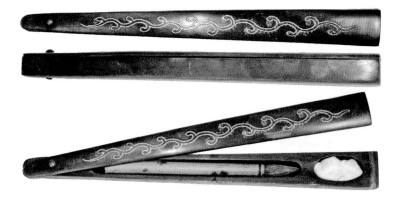

Figure 3. A *yatate* in the shape of a folded or closed fan. Portable writing sets like these were carried by samurai in their quivers along with their arrows so they could write letters and reports from the battlefield.

Figure 4. Popular with samurai and *chōnin* alike by the Edo period, *yatate* were by then more frequently shaped like a dipper with a hinged ink pot attached to one end.

Figure 5. This woodblock print by Katsushika Hokusai shows a *chōnin* lighting his tobacco pipe from a miniature charcoal brazier mounted in a tobacco tray. Note he also has a *yatate* tucked into his *obi* at his waist.

By the beginning of the Edo period, yatate were popular with both chōnin and samurai alike. To increase the capacity of the ink carried, most yatate were by then shaped like a *hishaku-gata* (dipper) with a round metal tube for holding a small writing brush and a *sumi tsubo* (hinged ink pot) to hold an ink-soaked cloth affixed to one end. The hinged lid allowed access to both the writing brush and the ink container. No longer associated with arrow stands yet retaining their original name, yatate were commonly carried tucked into the obi. Figure 4 is a example of the later popular form of yatate shaped like a hishaku-gata. Figure 5 illustrates how a samurai or chōnin typically carried a kiseru and yatate.

Kozuka and Kogatana

The *kozuka* is the handle for a *kogatana*, a small utility blade frequently carried in a small slot near the top of a wakizashi or *tanto saya* (scabbard). The kogatana are generally polished flat on one side and ground to a sharp edge on the opposite side, and have a small tang to fit inside the kozuka. These small utility knives were frequently referred to as kozuka or kozuka blades. Figure 6 shows a typical kozuka blade, a kogatana mounted in a kozuka.

While the kozuka was frequently decorated with precious metals and intricate designs, the simple-forged kogatana functioned as a general purpose knife or even as a small dagger. The young sons of

KOGATANA   **KOZUKA**

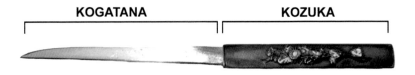

Figure 6. The *kozuka* is a decorative handle for a *kogatana*, a small utility knife blade with a tang that is inserted into the handle.

samurai families would often entertain themselves for hours by practicing their throwing skills with their kozuka blades. These small
utility knives could also be used in emergencies like shuriken, or
throwing knives, to momentarily distract or blind an attacker. Figure
7 shows several Edo-period kozuka and kogatana.

Figure 7. Slots in the scabbard of *wakizashi* and *tanto*
often held *kozuka* and *kogatana*, which formed the
handle and blade of a small auxiliary utility knife. Above
are three *kozuka* with *kogatana* and a decorative *kozuka*
without the matching blade.

Kogai

The samurai's wakizashi or tanto saya often included a second slot
to accommodate a *kogai*, a sort of skewer with a blunted tip.
Although the uses for the kozuka and kogatana as a general purpose
knife are fairly obvious, the intended purpose of the kogai remains
somewhat of a mystery. Some authorities have proposed that after a
head was removed on the battlefield, the kogai was thrust through
an opponent's ear so all would know who the victor was. In this
fashion, the kogai may have been used much like the kubizashi, a
small knife used by samurai on the battlefield to mark or even carry
the severed heads of enemy soldiers.

Figure 8. A typical *kogai* from the Edo period. The long blade may have been used to groom hair or scratch body areas through armor. The small scalloped-shaped protrusion was likely used to clean inside the ears.

Other historians believe the kogai may have been some sort of personal grooming item. The long blunt skewer-like blade could have been used by the samurai to push tufts of loose hair back into place in their elaborate hairstyles or to scratch areas of the body difficult to reach through small openings in their armor. The small scalloped-shaped protrusion at the opposite end of the kogai handle was likely used to clean the ears. Figure 8 shows an Edo period kogai.

A description of a kogai and its use is provided in *A Daughter of the Samurai*, written in 1928 by Etsu Inagaki Sugimoto, a Japanese language and history instructor at Columbia University. While traveling to Tokyo for a "modern" education, she and her brother stayed at the home of a former attendant to three women who defended a castle in a desperate but hopeless struggle. After listening to the old woman's story, the author described the kogai as follows:

> *Seeing that we were deeply interested, she brought out her other treasure—a slender, blunt knife called a kogai, which, with the throwing-dagger, forms part of the hilt of a samurai's long sword. In very ancient days Japanese warfare was a science. Artistic skill was always displayed in the use of weapons, and no soldier was proud of having wounded an enemy in any other manner than the one established by strict samurai rule. The long sword had for its goal only*

four points: the top of the head, the wrist, the side, and the leg below the knee. The throwing-dagger must speed on its way, true as an arrow, direct to the forehead, throat, or wrist. But the blunt little kogai had many uses. It was the key that locked the sword in its scabbard; when double it could be used as chopsticks by the marching soldier; it has been used on the battlefield, or in retreat, mercifully to pierce the ankle vein of a suffering and dying comrade, and it had the unique use in a clan feud, when found sticking upright in the ankle of a dead foe, of bearing the silent challenge, "I await thy return." Its crest told to whom it belonged and, in time, it generally was returned—to its owner's ankle. The kogai figures in many tales of romance and revenge of the Middle Ages.

The kogai is frequently considered a type of shuriken within a few classical martial arts traditions. However, the bluntness of the tip and the relatively small weight makes it doubtful the kogai could be used very effectively as a throwing knife.

Banshin

The *umagoya sangu*, or "three tools of the stable," included the *hana-neji* (nose screw), a short wooden stick and cord loop used to control horses; the *jingama* (camp sickle), a curved single-edged blade attached to a wooden handle used to clear campsites and to cut grasses for horse fodder; and another small knife frequently carried by samurai called the *banshin* or *umabari* (horse needle) used to bleed a horse's veins. After being ridden for extremely long distances, the veins in a horse's legs would fill with blood and sometimes become quite swollen. To relieve the pressure, the small bladed knives were used to puncture the veins and thus relieve the pressure. Unlike the kozuka and kogatana, the banshin were typically forged of iron in one solid piece and without any decoration. Yet a banshin in the hands of an expert could also be used as a shuriken when confronted by an attacker. Figure 9 shows a typical banshin.

Figure 9. Intended primarily for treating injured horses, *banshin* were typically forged of iron in one solid piece and without decoration.

Kanzashi

The *kanzashi* is a traditional hair ornament used in Japanese hairstyles. The kanzashi were first used as Japanese women abandoned their straight and long hairstyles and adopted coiffured *nihongami* hairstyles. When dressed formally, Japanese women usually wore one or more long pins, called kanzashi, hidden in their hair. Made from a wide range of materials—lacquered wood, gold and silver plated metal, tortoiseshell, and silk—kanzashi came into widespread use during the Edo period as artisans began to produce more finely crafted products.

There are many varieties and different styles of wearing kanzashi. The woman's status often dictated the specific type and fixed pattern of the kanzashi worn. Younger women usually wore more numerous and elaborate kanzashi than older or married women, for example.

Women from samurai families often trained to defend themselves with this rather extraordinary concealed weapon peculiar to their gender. Most kanzashi were several inches long, and while they served to keep a woman's long hair up and in place, the metal pins were also quite capable of piercing an attacker's chest or throat in an emergency. Figure 10 shows several different styles of kanzashi.

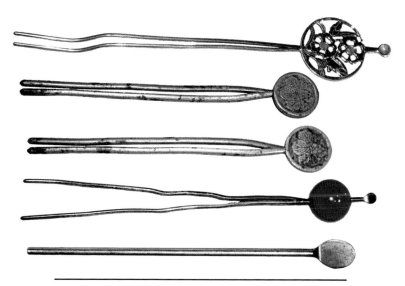

Figure 10. Made from a wide variety of materials, most *kanzashi* were several inches long and were quite capable of piercing an attacker's chest or throat in an emergency.

Tobikuchi

Most buildings in Edo were constructed of wood and paper. For heating and cooking, people depended on charcoal braziers and stoves. Oil lamps with open flames were often used for indoor lighting. As a result, there were many fires. In fact, fires were so common that they were known as *Edo no hana* (flowers of Edo).

During the early years, the various daimyō involved in building Edo and fortifying the castle also organized firefighting units, called the *daimyō hikeshi* (firemen), to protect the castle and their own manors. Later, the shōgun's retainers, the *hatamoto* (banner men), operated the *sada-bikeshi*, a similar group of firefighters, primarily to protect the castle. After a devastating fire in 1657, however, the machi-bugyō (town magistrate) took over responsibility for protecting Edo's citizens and property from fire and organized firefighting units, called the *machi-bikeshi* (town firemen), from the lowest classes of chōnin—the homeless, the unemployed, former criminals, and so on. The newly recruited professional firefighters, called *hikeshi*, were organized into *kumi* (units) and assigned to various geographical jurisdictions throughout the city.

Many of the hikeshi had formerly worked as *tobi-ninsōku*. The term *tobi* is a shortened version of *tobiguchi teko no mono*, or workers who use *teko* (a pulley and lever) such as carpenters, builders, plasterers, masons, and manual laborers. Whenever a fire broke out, the hikeshi would quickly tear down the burning structure and any surrounding houses or buildings to create firebreaks and prevent the flames from spreading.

To accomplish this task, the hikeshi carried a rather strange looking implement called a *tobikuchi*, apparently a reference to the blade shaped like a bird's beak. Similar to a fireman's axe, the tobikuchi was used to hook and pull down walls and screens. The hikeshi would use the sharp pointed blade to smash rounded tiles flat for creating footholds on the slippery roofs of buildings. A longer polearm version of the tobikuchi was used to pull down a building's main support beams.

In return for their services, the respective neighborhoods provided hikeshi with a small salary, work implements, and a suit of clothing made of a special thick woven cotton. When doused with water, this heavy clothing provided limited protection from burns. Although admired greatly by the common people for their courage and personal sacrifice, the city's firefighters also quickly earned a reputation for their course language, quick temper, and rough-and-tumble manners. Although it was primarily a working tool, the tobikuchi was also sometimes employed as an impromptu truncheon in street brawls.

Figure 11 shows a Meiji era tobikuchi cast of solid iron. Figure 12 is an earlier version made of an iron head affixed to a wooden handle bolstered with iron strips and bands. Figure 13 is an unusual polished steel jutte shaped like a miniature tobikuchi with engraved

Tokugawa *kamon* (crest) in silver at both ends. As such, this jutte was probably carried as a symbol of office by a hatamoto leader for one of the special fire brigades, called *jo hikeshi*.

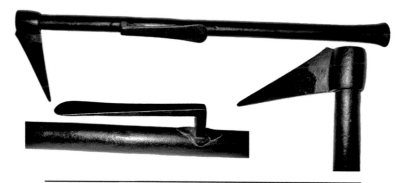

Figure 11. Edo-period *hikeshi* used a *tobikuchi* to quickly pull down screens and siding, often even the supporting beams. This *tobikuchi* is solid iron. Unlike the *jutte*, the long flat *kagi* (hook) was used to secure the *tobikuchi* in the *obi*.

Figure 12. This *tobikuchi* is wood with several iron bands. The forged iron head is engraved with a single kanji character.

Figure 13. This small polished steel *jutte* has a handle shaped as a miniature *tobikuchi*, the tool carried by *hikeshi*. The engraved *kamon* (crest) is the *aoi-no-mon* (three hollyhock leaves), symbol of the Tokugawa family, allowed to be displayed only by relatives and *hatamoto*. This *jutte* was likely carried as a symbol of office by a *hatamoto* leader for one of the special fire brigades, called *jo hikeshi*, organized by the government after the Meireki fire in 1657.

Shakuhachi

The strangest and most unlikely defensive weapon has to be the bamboo flute, known in Japan as the *shakuhachi*. The shakuhachi is an end-blown flute made from bamboo root and used in traditional Japanese music. The soulful and deeply moving music played on the shakuhachi is often associated with the practice of Zen Buddhism and meditation. The shakuhachi was popularized by the Fuke sect of Buddhism sometime in the thirteenth century. This sect sought to replace sutra chanting with *sui zen* (blowing zen) through the use of the shakuhachi.

During the Edo Period, which was marked by disintegration of feudal Japan, the shakuhachi was often favored by swelling numbers of uprooted and masterless samurai warriors, or rōnin. Large numbers of rōnin joined the ranks of itinerant preachers known as

Figure 14. Made from the bamboo root, the longer and stouter *shakuhachi* could also serve as a truncheon. The *tengai* is a basket-shaped hat worn by komoso that covered the entire face, thus also serving as a very effective disguise.

komuso (priests of emptiness and nothingness). The komuso were identified by the large *tengai* (woven basket-like hats) which they wore over their heads to symbolize their detachment from the world. In this way, they roamed from village to village, playing the shakuhachi and accepting alms.

The komuso may be the source of many stories of ninja, or feudal Japanese spies with near mystical powers and unusual weapons. Popular fiction often portrays ninja disguised as komuso, wearing their tengai which completely covered the face and head during the day, and their black suits and masks at night.

Violent clan struggles during the late sixteenth century forced many of the komuso to organize themselves into societies for self-protection. During the relative peace following the Sengoku period, the Tokugawa shōgun gave the members of these societies exclusive rights to play the shakuhachi and to solicit alms. In return for this privilege, the komuso agreed to spy on the activities of other rōnin, watching for any signs of a potential rebellion.

In any case, no longer part of the samurai class, komuso were forbidden to wear swords. According to legend, therefore, the komuso redesigned the shakuhachi from the root of bamboo. By making it longer and stouter, the shakuhachi could then also be used like a club. Figure 14 shows two shakuhachi and a tengai, the basket-shaped hat worn by komuso to cover and hide the face and head.

3

Hidden Weapons

There were many specialized and easily concealable weapons available for use when one was otherwise unarmed or, in some cases, when it was preferable not to kill or seriously maim the attacker. A wide range of specialized short arms were designed for both offense and self-defense purposes. These specialized weapons generally could be easily concealed within the everyday clothing of samurai and chōnin.

These weapons include items small enough to be hidden in the folds or sleeve of the kimono, tucked in the obi, or even concealed within the hand. This type of implement is often referred to as *hibuki* (hidden weapons). Another term sometimes used is *kakushibuki* (concealed weapon).

秘武器

hibuki

Many different Japanese traditional martial arts styles employed the use of weapons which were easily concealed. Japanese craftsmen found many ingenious methods to hide edged weapons, from knives hidden in fan cases to sword blades and spears in canes and walking sticks. In some cases, though, hibuki included hand load weapons designed for *atemi* (striking) at vital points or sensitive areas on an opponent's body. Other hidden weapons included weighted chain weapons which could be swung to strike an opponent or to entangle an attacker's weapon. There were also several concealed weapons which could be thrown to distract or blind an opponent.

Shikomibuki

The Japanese weapons craftsmen were very clever in constructing any number of *shikomibuki* (prepared weapons) that appeared innocuous to the casual, yet concealed hidden knife blades, sharp metal spikes, or even sword blades. While shikomibuki appeared to be rather inconspicuous everyday objects, these deceptive weapons allowed the bearer to surprise an opponent who mistakenly believed their victim was unarmed. The shikomibuki could easily be carried by samurai in situations when they were not allowed to openly bear arms, such as another person's home, a castle, or a tea room. Almost any item could conceal a blade, such as shikomi-jutte. Figure 15 and Figure 16 are two Edo period shikomi-jutte.

Because most commoners were banned from carrying bladed weapons, shikomibuki were often favored by those living on the fringes of society such as gamblers and criminals. The dangerous nature of their business often involved the potential for violence. The shikomibuki offered a means for offense or self-defense that would still pass the most casual inspection by law enforcement or their criminal associates.

Shikomibuki could take the form of nearly any item that someone might carry on their person. The shikomi kiseruzutsu looked like an ordinary pipe case, yet concealed a dagger or sharpened metal spike. Some even still functioned as a pipe case as well. The shikomi kiseru looked like a tobacco pipe, yet would hide a sharp spike or needle-like blade that could be used to pierce or stab an unsuspecting victim. The shikomi-yatate gave the impression of being a typical portable writing set, yet would hide a thin knife blade or sharpened spike. Flutes were another popular item serving as shikomibuki. Disguised as a small flute, the *shikomibue* was actually little more than a tanto (short knife) that could be carried in the obi without arousing suspicion.

The *shikomi-sensu* was a dagger hidden in a mounting made to appear as a closed fan. Because the fan was such a common item

Figure 15. This late Edo period *shikomi-jutte* features siver-inlay decorations on three sides of the six-sided iron *boshin*. The jutte has same on the *tsuka* and a small rectangular-shaped *tsuba* instead of a *kagi*. The *tsuka* unlocks from the *boshin* to reveal a hidden dagger. The *boshin* is also flared toward the sentan, adding weight to the striking end. The *kan* is attached to a copper or brass pommel on the *tsuka*. A *jutte* without a *kagi* was also referred to as *naeshi* or *nayashi*.

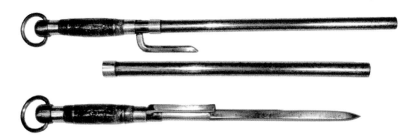

Figure 16. This is a late Edo period *shikomi-jutte* decorated with brass and silver. The *tsuka* is covered in lacquered *same*. This *shikomi-jutte* was probably carried by an *aratame* (official inspector) primarily for identification and as a symbol of office. However, a sharp blade of forged steel is hidden in the hollow round *boshin*.

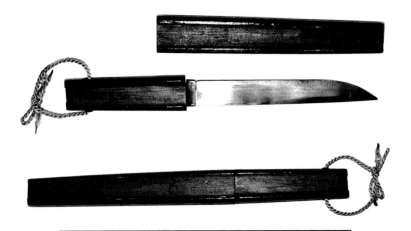

Figure 17. Japanese craftsmen often found ingenious methods to hide edged weapons. Above is an Edo period *shikomi-sensu*, a dagger disguised as a closed fan; it measures approximately 12 inches in length.

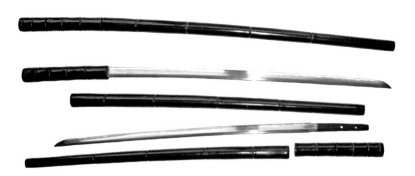

Figure 18. A *shikomijo* or cane sword. The blade is originally a sixteenth-century *tachi* (long sword) that has been remounted as a bamboo-shaped walking stick probably during the Meiji era.

carried by both samurai and chōnin, the shikomi-sensu was the favorite weapon of assassins, gamblers, and other criminals. Figure 17 shows an Edo period shikomi-sensu.

The *shikomijo* was a staff or cane made to conceal a sword blade. These were mostly carried by chōnin during the Edo period as walking sticks and were not usually carried by samurai unless they were elderly or feeble. However, the shikomijo or cane sword became quite popular among former samurai during the Meiji era. As Japan rushed to adopt Western technology and culture, the samurai class was abolished and the wearing of swords in public was banned. The cane was a common fashion accessory during the late nineteenth century in Western society, so it was not unusual for a well-dressed Japanese man to have one as well.

Despite the new laws against wearing swords, many former samurai still believed that it was their traditional right to be armed with a sword. Special shikomijo were constructed with hidden blades, or former sword blades were mounted in new *koshirae* (sword furniture) with the tsuka (hilt) and saya (scabbard) made to look like nothing more than a modern walking stick or cane. Figure 18 shows a typical Japanese style shikomijo.

Kongōsho

The *mikkyō hōgu* are utensils used in ritual incantation and prayer for *mikkyō* or the practices of esoteric Buddhism which was introduced to Japan during the early Heian period. One form of the utensils used in mikkyō is derived from an ancient Indian weapon. The *kongōsho*, sometimes referred to as a vajra (thunderbolt) club, is a pestle-like object with pointed ends. The kongōsho is typically made of gilt bronze with *kimoku* (goblin eyes) or *kimen* (goblin heads) around the central grip and an eight-petal lotus flower above and below the center. A symbolic item often seen in the hands of various guardian figures associated with mikkyō, the kongōsho represents the indestructibility of Buddhist law and the power of the Buddha to vanquish evil.

There are various types of kongōsho depending on the number and shape of the prongs at both ends. The oldest forms most frequently found in Japan are the *tokkosho* (single-pronged pestle), *sankosho* (three-pronged pestle), and *gokosho* (five-pronged pestle). The tokkosho is a single-point style frequently used in Shingon and Tendai mikkyō rituals. Usually carried by priests, itinerant monks, and religious pilgrims for their spiritual ceremonies, the tokkosho could also serve as an emergency self-defense weapon against bandits or thieves. Figure 19 shows a Japanese style tokkosho.

The use of the tokkosho as a fighting weapon for atemi, or striking arts, certainly caught the attention of the samurai. The tokkosho was employed in several martial arts traditions, most notably Shorinji Kempo, a form of Chinese-style boxing. Many believe the tokkosho is also the precursor for several types of hand load weapons and fighting techniques taught in many other classical jūjutsu *ryūha* or styles.

Figure 19. A *kongōsho*. This style is called a *tokkosho* due to the single prongs on both ends. The *tokkosho* was employed in several classical martial arts traditions, most notably Shorinji Kempo, a form of Chinese-style boxing.

Yawara-bō

Many jūjutsu schools taught the use of a short wooden rod which could be held in the hand, extending slightly from each end of the fist. This commonly carried hibuki was called the *yawara-bō*, sometimes referred to simply as a yawara. The first kanji character, *yawara*, means "flexibility" or "giving way." The same kanji character is also pronounced as "jū" in Japanese terms like jūdō or jūjutsu. The second kanji character, *bō*, simply means "stick." The yawara-bō was also occasionally referred to as *tenouchi*, literally meaning something "inside the hand."

yawara-bō

The yawara-bō was basically a short wooden rod used as a hand load weapon to maximize body strikes as well as to block an adversary's blows or kicks. The wooden shaft was also frequently carved to better fit the user's fingers and to improve grip. The yawara-bō

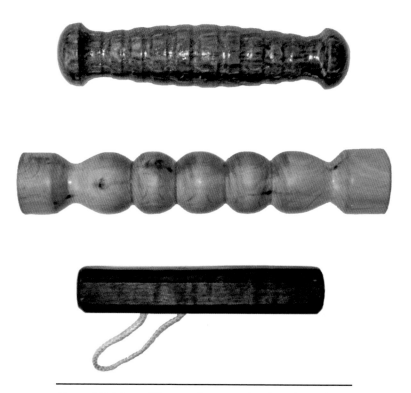

Figure 20. Many different shapes and styles of wooden *yawara-bō* are readily available from most any martial arts store.

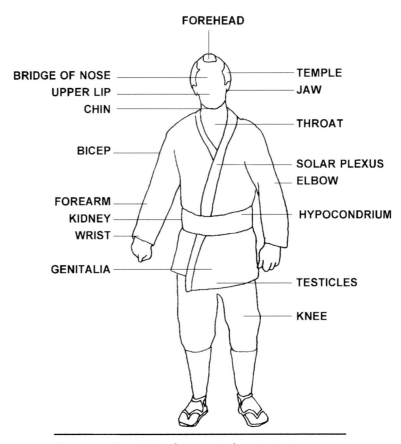

Figure 21. The *kyūsho* (vital points) on the body that could be easily targeted at close range with a strike from a *yawara-bō*.

generally measured from around 5 to 8 sun in length, or 6 to 10 inches (18 to 30 centimeters).

Some historians believe that yawara-bō techniques were developed by samurai from tanto-jitsu or short knife fighting techniques. According to the theory, the saya (scabbard) for the short blade might swell due to moisture from rain, humidity, or perspiration, making it difficult for the samurai to draw the blade free. If this occurred, the samurai would resort to using the tanto saya as a weapon. Another view is that samurai might have used the tanto saya when a more deadly weapon was not necessary.

The yawara-bō more likely evolved from the use of tokkosho by Buddhist priests, itinerant monks, and religious pilgrims who carried such ritual items for use in esoteric incantations and prayer. Many found that the tokkosho not only symbolized the power of the Buddha to vanquish evil, but served equally well as a hand-held weapon in self defense against thieves and bandits. Because metal was very expensive and required special tools and skills to forge utensils, wood was a more practical alternative and far easier to obtain. Anyone could simply carve a yawara-bō from whatever wood was readily available. Figure 20 shows several types of yawara-bō made of wood.

The yawara-bō was typically held in either hand, extending slightly from both ends of the fist. Gripped in this manner, the yawara-bō could then be used either to hit at or to apply concentrated pressure against an opponent's *kyūsho* (vital points), the sensitive nerve centers on an opponent's body. Held across the palm, the yawara-bō could also be used to block strikes or blows, even knife and sword slashes. Figure 21 shows the kyūsho that could be targeted with yawara-bō.

Because the yawara-bō is so easy to make and to use, various styles have been introduced for self-defense in the West. A Japanese immigrant, Frank Matsuyama was a full-time yawara-jitsu instructor in the 1930s for the Berkeley, California, police department. As described in his book *How to Use the Yawara Stick for Police*, Matsuyama developed an updated version of the yawara-bō during the late 1940s which proved quite popular for use in law enforcement. Made of hard Bakelite plastic, Matsuyama's yawara stick included several golf shoe spikes mounted in the ends. The short metal spikes were intended to discourage someone from grabbing the yawara stick from the officer's hand or to inflict additional pain when necessary to control a suspect. Figure 22 shows a yawara stick designed

Figure 22. This is the *yawara* stick that was developed by Frank Matsuyama for law enforcement use in the late 1940s. It is made of hard Bakelite plastic with golf shoe spikes mounted in the ends. The words "Yawara School" and "Denver, Colo" are engraved on both ends.

Figure 23. Modern technology and materials have resulted in any number of *yawara-bō* being developed as self-defense weapons for the general public. The *yawara-bō* at top is made of hard nylon. The two below are made from aircraft grade aluminum.

by Matsuyama specifically for police use. Figure 23 shows several other modern versions of yawara-bō made of high-tech materials and marketed as self-defense weapons to the general public.

Suntetsu

Similar to the wooden yawara-bō, a forged iron tenouchi was called *suntetsu*. The first kanji character, *sun*, is a unit of measurement. The second kanji character, *tetsu*, simply means "iron." As the name implies, the suntetsu consisted of a short iron bar. This metal implement could be used in the hand in much the same manner as the short wooden rod. Due to the heavier weight of the iron bar, the suntetsu could also be thrown to distract or even injure an attacker.

寸
鉄

suntetsu

Suntetsu sometimes include a short loop of rope or a metal ring. Worn around the middle finger, the ring allows the suntetsu to pivot

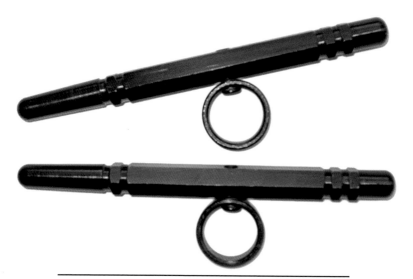

Figure 24. The steel *suntetsu* includes a metal ring which is worn around the middle finger. When the *suntetsu* is gripped in the palm, the ring allows it to pivot inside the hand so different grips may be used.

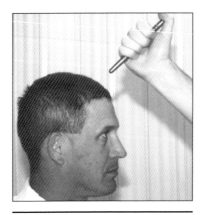

Figure 25.

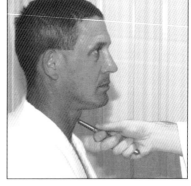

Figure 26.

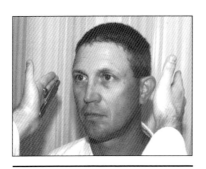

Figure 27.

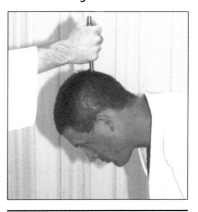

Figure 28.

Figure 29.

Figure 30.

Figure 31.

Figure 32.

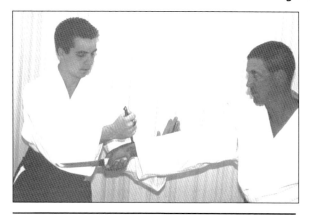

Figure 33.

inside the hand so different grips may be used. This also allows it to be used for palm strikes and blocks against cuts with edged weapons. Figure 24 shows a suntetsu made of steel with metal rings used to switch grips without losing the weapon.

Like the tenouchi or yawara-bō, the suntetsu can be used to strike sensitive nerve points or to block against an attack. Figure 25 through Figure 33 illustrate how suntetsu can be used to strike at an opponent's sensitive nerve points from different directions, to block an attack, or to parry an edged weapon.

Manriki-kusari

万
力
鎖

manriki-kusari

Dannoshin Toshimitsu Masaki, a samurai serving as the head sentry at Edo castle, allegedly developed the short weighted-chain weapon that is called a *manriki-kusari* (ten-thousand-power chain) sometime during the early eighteenth century. A member of the Toda clan, Masaki was appointed guardian for the Otemon Gate at Edo castle. According to legend, Masaki created this unusual weapon to prevent needless bloodshed should the guards be required to defend the castle from intruders. Since blood was considered spiritually unclean, this may have been less for humane reasons than to protect the sacred areas they guarded from being defiled.

The manriki-kusari was made from a short length of metal chain, about two to three feet long, with weights on each end. The chain was useful for parrying strikes from sticks and swords, and the weights could be swung to strike an opponent or tangle a weapon.

Figure 34. The *manriki-kusari* (ten-thousand power chain) was also referred to as *fundo-kusari* (weighted chain), *sode-kusari* (sleeve-chain), and *kusari-jutte* (chain-truncheon), as well as many other names.

Figure 35.

Figure 36.

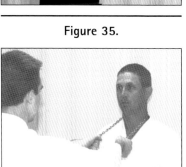

Figure 37.

Figure 38.

The manriki-kusari was later adopted by many samurai to disarm and capture criminals. It was also referred to as fundō-kusari (weighted chain), sode-kusari (sleeve-chain), and kusari-jutte (chain-truncheon). Figure 34 shows two manriki-kusari with different shaped weights.

分
銅
鎖

fundo-kusari

Figure 35 and Figure 36 illustrate how the manriki-kusari can be used to parry strikes from sticks, swords, or other weapons. Figure 37 and Figure 38 show a manriki-kusari being used to capture and throw an opponent.

Kusurigama

During the early part of the Edo period, many samurai favored the *bō* (wooden staff) and the *kusurigama*, a short sickle with a weighted chain attached. Unlike the farmer's tool for harvesting grain, the kusurigama evolved from a unique tool called a *jingama* (camp sickle) carried mainly by low-ranking bushi in earlier times. Much like its agricultural counterpart, the jingama has a curved single-edged blade attached to a wooden handle. As one of the *umagoya sangu* (three tools of the stable), it was primarily used by the samurai to clear campsites, cut grasses for horse fodder, and perform other utilitarian camp tasks.

The jingama was worn either stuck in the obi near the small of the back or slung over the back. Because it was easy to access, the

Figure 39. An Edo period *kusarigama*, a short sickle with a weighted chain attached. The handle is covered in *raden*, a traditional Japanese lacquer wood inlay using mother-of-pearl fragments from oyster shells. It also has decoratively engraved copper fittings. With the *kusurigama* held in one hand, the chain and weight could be swung with the other hand to distract or force an opponent away, to strike, or to entangle a weapon.

jingama was also a convenient weapon in case of a surprise attack. The way the blade is attached to the wooden handle allowed the weapon to be used for cutting and slashing, and even for thrusting in a stabbing motion.

The wooden handle of the kusurigama was frequently reinforced with metal bands or strips. Many were also fitted with metal hand-guards as well, again at either end of the handle. The weighted chain added to the jingama to complete the kusurigama was most likely derived from the *konbi*, a Chinese weapon. Depending on the school, the variable-length chain was linked to the handle at either end or even in the middle. Holding the kusurigama in one hand, the samurai could swing the chain and weight with the other hand in a circular motion to distract or force an opponent to keep away, to strike an opponent, or to entangle and ensnare an opponent's weapon. Figure 39 shows an Edo period kusarigama.

Shuriken

The *shuriken* (hand-hidden blade) was a concealed weapon used for throwing and sometimes for stabbing. Although not much is known about the origins of these small throwing weapons, most shuriken were small, sharpened, hand-held blades or spikes made from a variety of common items. There were two basic styles, the *bo shuriken* and the *shaken*. Easily concealing these in the folds of their clothing or obi, the samurai could quickly throw one or more shuriken at the exposed parts of an enemy's body to injure or distract their opponent.

Bo shuriken are long, thin, and cylindrical, with varying thicknesses and shapes. The *hari gata* (needle shape) were likely created from needles or hole punches used for stitching cloth and leather, or for lacing armor. The *kugi gata* (nail shape) were thicker and usually square. These were likely created from the square metal *wakugi* (nails), ranging from the small nails used for furniture to large metal rods used in the support beams of buildings. Finally, the *tanto gata* (knife shape) were flatter and wider, with a sharp pointed shape like a knife blade.

Shaken, sometimes referred to as kurumaken, were made from flat pieces of metal and fashioned into sharp edged, concealable weapons of varying shapes and sizes. (This type of shuriken has been popularized as the "throwing star" or "ninja star.") These may have been constructed from small pieces of armor plate or from the flat metal fittings used in building construction. The shaken could be thrown at the exposed face or arms of an opponent. Gripped in the hand, the shaken could also be used to stab or slash at an enemy.

Some believe the use of shuriken originally involved throwing various cooking implements, such as *hanshi* (eating sticks) or *hibashi*, metal tongs used to tend small cooking and heating fires. Others believe kogai or kozuka and kogatana were used as improvised throwing weapons. There are many stories of samurai throwing, or even spitting, needles into the faces of their opponents.

Metsubushi

In addition to their various arresting and defensive weapons, feudal-era samurai also sometimes employed a wide range of clever *metsubushi* (sight removers) to distract and confuse their adversaries. Ingredients used for metsubushi were not intended to permanently damage the eyes. The purpose was simply to startle an opponent, however briefly. A moment of confusion created by a blinding attack was typically sufficient to either close the distance and use another weapon or to hide and evade an opponent.

Nearly any form of irritating powder or liquid could be used as metsubushi. It might be as simple as grabbing a handful of whatever was convenient, such as dirt, sand, pebbles, ashes, water, or cooking oil, and tossing it into an opponent's face. In some cases, specific ingredients for metsubushi, such as dried and ground hot peppers, nettles, even small charge explosives and smoke, were prepared in advance. In the latter case, special hollow containers were necessary to hold and carry the metsubushi until it was ready to be employed. Empty eggshells, nut shells, and short lengths of bamboo were all effectively used as containers for prepared metsubushi.

A special, often rather ornate container was the *sokutōku*. Worn around the neck like a necklace, it provided an effective means of blinding an opponent with a single breath. The hollowed device was usually filled with fine sand boiled in a solution of red peppers, then plugged with a stopper attached by a short, thin cord. When needed, the user merely brought the sokutōku to his mouth, removed the plug from the opposite end by tugging on the cord, and blew sharply into the mouthpiece. A cloud of small hot-peppered sand particles were then sprayed into the adversary's eyes, blinding him with intense pain. Figure 40 shows an ornate Edo period sokutōku.

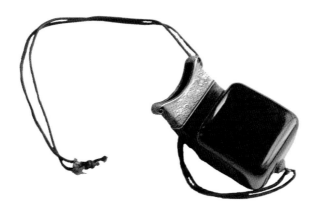

Figure 40. This ornate *sokutōku* held the *metsubushi* until needed by the early police officers to distract and confuse their adversaries when making arrests. *(From the collection of Nawa Yumio)*

Hojo-jutsu

Once an opponent was subdued in close-quarter grappling, it was then necessary to restrain the individual so he could be confined without posing a risk of further injury. Frequently, binding had to be done quickly, so feudal-era samurai developed very sophisticated methods to bind prisoners in such cases. The resulting restraining arts were generally referred to as *hojo-jutsu*. Figure 41 shows many complicated binding patterns for restraining different social classes developed by the feudal Japanese police. Specific binding patterns were used for nobles, samurai, farmers, artisans, merchants, monks, priests, and beggars. A special pattern, called *chigo-nawa*, was used for restraining children. There were also three different restraining patterns developed for women—*onnagoho*, *chichi-hazushi*, and *chichikake-nawa*—each designed specifically to protect their breasts.

Torinawa (Arresting Ropes)

Special ropes were used in hojo-jutsu, sometimes with barbed metal hooks or loops tied on one end. The barbed metal hooks were intended to catch in the victim's clothing. The cord loops or metal rings were often used instead of actual knots to bind the suspect so that the person was not humiliated by being bound. Binding some-one without employing knots apparently avoided the disgrace associated with bondage. Simple euphemisms such as "wrapping" were thus often employed in this case to describe their situation.

The *torinawa* (arresting ropes) were of various lengths, based on the particular ryūha or style. The different binding techniques were also either simple or complicated and not standardized among differ-ent schools. Samurai officials would frequently carry a torinawa under their obi or hidden loosely inside their jackets. Often they would carry a torinawa tucked inside their kimono sleeve, with one end already wrapped around their own wrist. From here, it was fairly easy to grasp the torinawa and quickly secure their prisoner. Even everyday clothing items could be used as a torinawa in an

捕
縄

torinawa

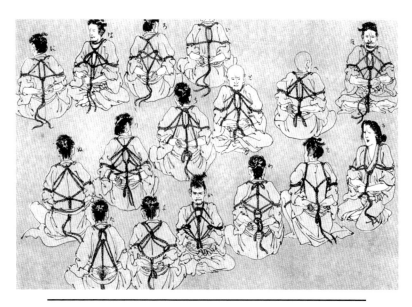

Figure 41. The feudal Japanese police developed many complicated binding patterns for different social classes. Specific binding patterns were developed for nobles, samurai, farmers, artisans, merchants, monks, priests, and beggars. *(Illustration from Tokugawa Bakufu Keiji Zufu Kan [Pictorial Book on Tokugawa Government Penal Affairs] by Shinataro Fujita, 1893)*

Figure 42. The wife of a samurai restrains a burglar by using her *obi jime*, a cord used to hold the *obi* in place when worn with a *kimono*, in this woodblock illustration by Kuniyōshi.

emergency. Figure 42 is a woodblock print by Kuniyōshi illustrating the wife of a samurai restraining a burglar with her *obi jime*, the cord that holds the obi in place when worn with a kimono.

Arai Hakuseki (1657–1725), chief counselor for the sixth shōgun, Tokugawa Ienobu, was a very learned man with a wide range of interests. He authored many books, and his autobiographical *Oritaku Shiba no Ki* [Breaking and Burning Firewood] is best known for its portrait of his father, Masanari.

In the opening sections, he describes a childhood incident involving a torinawa which accidentally dropped from his kimono.

Particularly interesting is the disdain his father reveals for the physical act of arresting and restraining criminals. Like many of his contemporaries, he felt this was beneath the dignity of a samurai. Arai Hakuseki recalls his father's advice as follows:

> *When I was seventeen or eighteen, I happened to drop in front of my father what was called an "arresting cord," which was used to tie up a man and was made of slender blue strings braided together, with a hook attached at its end, and which I then had in my breast.*
>
> *"What is this?" my father said and picked it up. After a while he said, "When I still held my former post, I used to carry one like this in my flint bag. That's because when there was someone who'd committed a crime, I would have my subordinates arrest him. I carried one in case they happened not to have one with them.*
>
> *"After I was freed from my post, it became useless, so I used it to tie a cat. I don't have to tell you that you must learn all the warrior's skills. But there are skills that you must practice according to your station, and there are skills that you must not. This is not the kind of implement you should carry with you. You are not so young as not to realize something as simple as this."*

The torinawa actually used were usually made of hemp. Silk ropes were apparently often used for practice. While the smoother silk ropes were easy to quickly tie and untie during training, the knots were too likely to slip in actual use. Therefore, torinawa were usually made of strong hemp fibers twisted by threes into a thin rope. Some historians claim that torinawa were then soaked in blood to prevent decay. Special short ropes were also used to secure the fingers and sometimes even the toes of prisoners. Figure 43 shows an Edo period torinawa.

Often tenouchi also incorporated a short length of rope or cord. Looped around the wrist, the cord allowed the tenouchi to be thrown to distract an opponent. With the cord attached to the wrist, the tenouchi is then easily retrieved. The cord loop could also be used to ensnare a person's limb or weapon as well as to restrain an attacker after they had been subdued. Figure 44 shows a tenouchi with a cord attached.

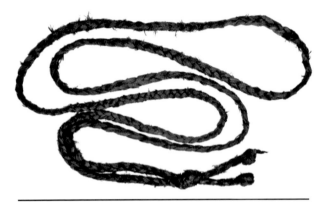

Figure 43. This Edo-period *torinawa* (arresting rope) or *torihimo* (arresting cord) is a hand-woven dark green rope made from hemp fibers.

Figure 44. Sometimes a short loop of cord was also attached to the *tenouchi* and used to ensnare and restrain an opponent.

Figure 45. By stretching the cord from one hand to the other, the cord may be used to wrap around an opponent's limbs or neck.

Figure 46. By looping the cord over the same hand, the cord may then be used like a snare by slipping the wrist back through the loop.

Figure 47. The opponent attacks with a knife to the stomach.

Figure 48. Avoid the attack by sidestepping forward with the left foot and strike the opponent's wrist with the *tenouchi* to make him drop the knife.

Figure 49. Slip the cord loop over the opponent's wrist and strike him in the face with the end of the *tenouchi*.

Figure 50. Then snare the opponent's wrist by slipping the *tenouchi* back through the cord loop.

Figure 51. To finish, use the *tenouchi* to bend the opponent's arm back at the elbow.

Figure 52. Then move behind the opponent, twisting his arm in a bent armbar.

Figure 53. Finish by looping the remaining cord over the opponent's head and use the *tenouchi* as a fulcrum to apply a choke and control the opponent.

Figure 54. For an alternate finish, step with the left foot onto the extended cord, forcing the opponent to the ground.

Figure 55. Then twist his arm into a bent armbar behind his back.

Figure 56. Finish by looping the remaining cord around the opponent's free hand and use your left arm to pull the cord tight and bind the opponent's wrists.

The cord could be stretched from one hand to the other as shown in Figure 45. In this way, it may be used to wrap around an opponent's limbs or neck. Another method was to loop the cord over the same hand as shown in Figure 46. The cord could then be used like a snare by slipping the wrist back through the loop. Figure 47 through Figure 56 show basic applications for the tenouchi and cord.

Hojokuwa

The *hojokuwa* (arresting ring) is often mistakenly believed to have been a *kakushibuki* or concealed weapon, but was more likely used for seizing and restraining an opponent. Sometimes called kakuke (horned hand), kakushi (horned finger), or kakuwa (horned ring), the hojokuwa was generally a small solid iron ring with anywhere from one to four or more sharp metal points or spikes. Figure 57 shows several different styles of hojokuwa.

There is no information available about the hojokuwa or how these were actually intended to be used, thus leading many to believe they were used for atemi with the sharp spikes facing outward to stab and injure an opponent struck by the knuckles. Several others have speculated that the hojokuwa may have been worn with the sharp points inward to hide it. The hojokuwa could then be used in much the same way by slapping the opponent with the palm of the hand.

The iron rings were probably worn on the middle fingers with the sharp spikes pointed inward toward the palm. If two were used, a second might be worn on the thumb. Wearing the hojokuwa with the

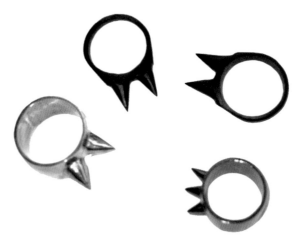

Figure 57. The *hojokuwa* (arresting ring) is often mistakenly believed to have been a *kakushibuki* or concealed weapon, but was more likely used for seizing and restraining an opponent.

sharp spikes facing into the palm was unlikely intended for conceal-ment, though. Worn in this manner, the sharp spines penetrated the opponent's clothing or flesh when gripping their garments or limbs, thus allowing the wearer to gain a much firmer hold. If seizing the victim by the arm or throat, the sharp pointed spikes would certainly cause a degree of pain and discomfort, yet the spikes were much too short to inflict serious injury.

4

Sensu and Tessen

Both the samurai and chōnin considered the hand fan an important fashion accessory and were rarely without one in any social situation. Although a hand fan was obviously useful for cooling oneself during the summer heat, the Japanese employed their fans for much more than just this simple utilitarian purpose. A fan was an ornament as well as a useful implement for illustrating a particular point or directing another person's attention.

The flat hand fan has been used since ancient times to create a cooling breeze. Early Japanese flat hand fans were probably inspired by the shape of leaves or a bird's wing. By the seventh century, the *sensu* (folding fan) was very popular at the Japanese court and among the early nobility. Folding fans were soon part of the performing arts of nō (masked drama) and buyo (Japanese classical dance) and even the tea ceremony. The folding fan was also an important element of court etiquette, and any samurai of high rank was required to know just how to hold or to wear his sensu in all situations he might encounter with various other officials.

Sensu

The earliest versions of sensu, hinoki fans, were made of thin slats of Japanese cypress hinoki wood that were stacked and bound.

Later, fans were created by pasting paper to a skeleton of split bamboo. These quickly evolved from the basic folding fan with the use of elegantly painted designs and paper sprinkled with gold and silver foil. Since then, many types of folding fans have been created with various materials, shapes, and decorations as times and tastes have changed. Figure 58 shows several typical Japanese sensu.

Figure 58. The Japanese *sensu* or folding fan is a practical device with beauty of both form and function.

Japanese merchants would even use their sensu as an appointment book or ledger. They would frequently write important notes about their schedule or other business-related issues on their personal folding fan where it was always handy for later reference. Among the cultural elite, a sensu was also often used to record an original verse of poetry by brushing the characters directly on the fan. These were especially valued as gifts.

Japanese women would often use their open fan to hide their expression, especially if it was considered impolite to reveal their

Figure 59. A folding fan was a required accessory for men as shown in this wedding photograph from approximately 1900.

sentiments in a particular situation. A sensu was an especially useful tool for flirtations, when certain terms or facial expressions could be used behind the screen of an open fan without being considered impolite. The open sensu was also used to conceal behavior considered socially offensive; for example, it was employed to cover the mouth when laughing or when chewing food.

For men, though, a folding fan was an accessory customarily carried in the hands or tucked in the obi, particularly when wearing ceremonial dress. Figure 59 shows the groom dressed in formal wear and holding a folding fan. The folding fan also played a significant role in Japanese etiquette, especially on formal occasions, and was rarely ever out of a samurai's possession. During the Edo Period, a retainer without his ever-present fan would be as incomplete as if he were not wearing his daishō, the customary set of two samurai swords that served as a badge of the warrior class.

Tessen

鉄
扇

tessen

In special cases, samurai would carry a *goshinki* (self-defense weapon) in addition to their daishō. Because a sensu was considered such a commonplace item, it seems quite natural that samurai and chōnin would eventually find that a hand fan made a suitable side arm with only some slight modifications. The *tessen*, literally meaning "iron fan," was either an actual folding fan with iron ribs or a non-folding solid bar made of either iron or wood and shaped like a folded fan. Solid tessen, forged from iron or carved from hard wood to look like a closed fan, were more durable and less expensive to make. Most considered the solid tessen more effective in combat than the folding style, making it quite popular with samurai, as well as the yakuza, otokodate, and machi-yakko from the chōnin ranks. The larger folding tessen quickly became a symbol of authority, while the smaller folding and solid tessen were a common self-defense weapon for extraordinary situations.

The samurai was often disarmed, such as when performing domestic chores, at leisure, or meeting with his superiors. If visiting another person's home, for example, a warrior was generally required to leave one or both swords with an attendant. Those who were not members of the samurai class were typically forbidden to carry a sword. To prevent violence, obvious weapons such as swords, daggers, and spears were also strictly prohibited within the small confines of the pleasure districts such as Yoshiwara in Edo. Armed with a tessen in his obi, though, the samurai or chōnin was never completely unarmed. He could easily defend himself in an emergency with what appeared to be an ordinary, everyday object.

Figure 60. A seated samurai uses his *tessen* to block an attacker's short sword in this woodblock illustration.

Figure 60 shows a drawing of a samurai using his tessen to block an attack with a short sword.

Tessen Styles

The typical tessen varied from ten sun to one shaku long or approximately 10 to 12 inches (30 to 36 centimeters). The defensive applications of tessen-jutsu and jutte-jutsu (techniques using a feudal Japanese police iron truncheon) can also be employed with either a short wooden stick or metal rod.

Like Japanese hand fans, tessen were made in three basic shapes. In general, the three standard tessen shapes included the basic folding fan style, called *sensu-gata*; the style used for traditional Japanese dancing and in kabuki plays, called *maiōgi-gata*; and the shape which was used to control military troops during war, called *gunsen-gata*.

Figure 61 illustrates the three basic shapes of sensu and tessen. Figure 62 shows modern tessen in the sensu-gata (basic fan) shape. Figure 63 is an Edo period tessen, very plain with no decoration. Figure 64 is a seventeenth-century tessen in the shape of maiōgi-gata, a fan used in traditional Japanese dancing. Figure 65 is a modern tessen in the gunsen-gata or military shape.

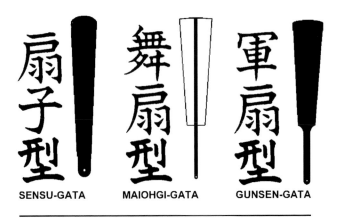

SENSU-GATA   **MAIOHGI-GATA**   **GUNSEN-GATA**

Figure 61. Three basic styles and the distinctive shapes of Japanese folding fans.

Figure 62. A pair of modern *tessen* in the *sensu-gata* or basic fan shape. Known as *menhari-gata*, the outer metal ribs protect the inner bamboo ribs.

Figure 63. An Edo period *tessen*. This iron *menhari-gata* is in the *sensu-gata* style.

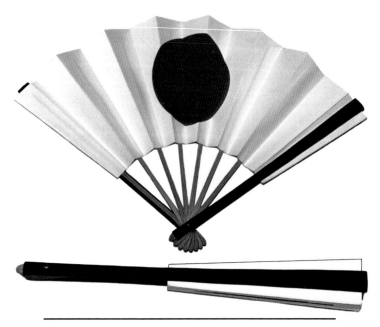

Figure 64. A folding *tessen* of the *menhari-gata* type. The outer ribs are made of iron while the inner ribs are made of bamboo. This seventeenth-century tessen is in the shape of *maiōgi-gata,* a fan used in traditional Japanese dancing.

微
直
物
menhari-gata

Tessen which actually folded were also referred to as menhari-gata. These were made of metal ribs covered with silk or washi, a very strong Japanese-style paper. The paper was often lacquered, reinforced with gold or silver foil, or treated with oil to make it both more decorative and less susceptible to weather damage. In some cases, only the outside ribs were metal while the inside ribs were made of the more flexible and lightweight bamboo strips. The latter were less heavy and easier to carry than the former, but were only effective as a self-defense implement when closed.

A folding tessen was not only effective as a defensive weapon, but could obviously be used as a regular hand fan if necessary. The ribs were held by a pin called a *kaname,* a term which is still used

Figure 65. This modern *tessen* is in the *gunsen-gata* or military shape. Both the outer and inner ribs are made of metal, then lacquered with a high gloss.

today in Japan to refer to the "main point" or to a "key individual." Although the dual functionality provided an evident advantage, this type could be expensive to make and difficult to maintain. In most cases, though, the term tessen was used to refer to the folding style.

kaname

As an alternative, some tessen called *tenarashi-gata* were made of solid iron cast in the shape of a closed fan. Some of these tenarashi-gata were made with very straight edges and only faintly resembled a typical hand fan while others were more convincing replicas of a closed fan. Figure 66 shows three Edo period tenarashi-gata tessen forged in iron in the shape of maiōgi-gata, a fan used in traditional Japanese dancing.

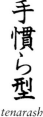

tenarashi-gata

Figure 66. These are three Edo period *tenarashi-gata*, non-folding *tessen* cast of iron, designed in the shape of closed *maiōgi-gata* (fans used in traditional Japanese dancing). The top one has a rattan-wrapped *tsuka*. Formerly part of a collection from Kanazawa in Ishikawa prefecture, the middle example is made of heavy square section iron. A *torinawa* (arresting rope) made of hand-woven dark green rope was originally secured to and wrapped around the handle. The basic form and crude workmanship indicates the bottom example was made by a low-ranking craftsman.

motsu-shaku

Another style of solid tessen was carved from hard wood such as sunuke or oak. Called *motsu-shaku*, the solid wooden fan was fairly easy and inexpensive to make. In comparison to the heavier iron counterparts, a motsu-shaku was also lighter and therefore more convenient to carry in the obi. Samurai would often carry a motsu-shaku for self-protection as well as for practicing their martial art skills. Figure 67 shows two styles of motsu-shaku, or tessen carved

Figure 67. Solid *tessen* carved from wood, called *motsu-shaku*, were less expensive and easier to carry. The one on top is an Edo period *motsu-shaku*. The lower one is a modern version used for martial arts practice.

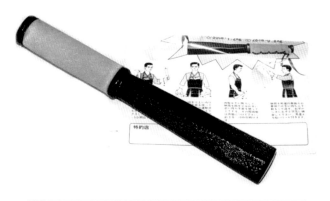

Figure 68. This very plain style *tenarashi-gata tessen* is currently sold in Japan for exercises to strengthen the wrists for *kendō*.

from wood. Figure 68 is a modern cast iron tenarashi-gata tessen used to exercise and strengthen the wrists for kendō.

There are numerous legends regarding individual combat involving the use of a tessen. One of the best known stories in Japanese folklore involved the heroes of many Japanese sagas, Minamoto Yoshitsune and his faithful retainer, Benkei. Probably the most popular Japanese historical figure of the period, Yoshitsune and his romantic exploits captured the imagination of the Japanese people, who have perpetuated numerous legends, stories, and kabuki plays. Born into the Minamoto family, a powerful military clan of imperial descent, Yoshitsune allegedly learned kenjutsu and tessen-jutsu secrets from *tengu*, mythical beings who were supposed to be expert martial artists.

After defeating and killing Yoshitsune's father, Minamoto Yoshitomo, during the Heiji Disturbance (1159), Taira Kiyomori spared the defeated leader's infant son, placing him in the care of Buddhist priests living in a monastery near Kyoto. As a teenager, though, Yoshitsune ran away from the monastery to join his older half-brother, Minamoto Yoritomo, in the Honshu region of northern Japan. During his travels in the mountain country, Yoshitsune was allegedly befriended by Sōjōbō, the king of tengu, who taught him the martial arts, including kenjutsu and tessen-jutsu, as well as military tactics that would serve him so well in his future exploits.

The tengu are described in ancient Japanese writings as something like mayhem-loving goblins. The tengu were supposedly fond of stealing peasant children and delighted in tormenting Buddhist priests. Although the mythical creatures took several forms, the most common variety, called *karasu*, combined human and crow-like characteristics.

The tengu were also often depicted as wearing the strangely shaped *tokin* (caps) and carrying the *shakujō* (ring-tipped staffs) of the wandering yamabushi, or ascetic mountain warriors. The yamabushi's tokin doubled as a drinking cup and the shakujō could be used to trap and even break spear or sword blades. Figure 69 and Figure 70 are illustrations of tengu practicing and teaching their martial arts skills.

Figure 69. Considered to be experts in the martial arts, *tengu* are shown above practicing unarmed and sword fighting skills. The *karasu* variety of *tengu* combined human and crow-like characteristics.

Figure 70. According to Japanese legends and myths, *tengu* would occasionally teach swordsmanship to a samurai.

Whether it was actually a tengu king or a kindly yamabushi hermit that served as his martial arts instructor, Yoshitsune was definitely an accomplished swordsman and military strategist. His tessen-jutsu skills, though, were to play a major role when Yoshitsune first encountered Benkei, a yamabushi of prodigious strength, on the Gojōbashi (Gojō bridge) in Kyoto.

Figure 71. Minamoto Yoshitsune avoids the slash of Benkei's razor-sharp *naginata* by jumping up onto the side railing of the *Gojōbashi* in this woodblock print by Kuniyōshi.

According to the legend, Benkei was a yamabushi of prodigious size and exceptional strength. The famous swordsmith Kokaji Munenobu had promised to forge a suit of armor and weapons suitable for Benkei's size and strength in exchange for one thousand swords. Armed with a naginata (a long pole arm or halbard), Benkei would nightly challenge samurai passersby to duels on the Gojōbashi.

Holding samurai in disdain, Benkei refused to let any pass without paying a duty. After defeating or intimidating his unfortunate adversaries, Benkei would take their swords as his prize. Benkei was reputed to be only a single sword short of his considerable undertaking when he met 18-year-old Yoshitsune accompanied by his servant, Kisanda, as they approached the bridge one night. Figures 71 and 72 are woodblock prints showing their fateful meeting that evening on the Gojōbashi.

As the youthful Yoshitsune started to cross the bridge, Benkei gruffly challenged him to a duel. Using the extraordinary agility he had learned from the tengu, Yoshitsune deftly avoided the deadly slash of Benkei's razor-sharp naginata by jumping up onto the bridge's side railing. Without drawing his own sword, Yoshitsune ultimately disarmed the much larger and stronger yamabushi by striking Benkei's wrist with a tessen, thus foiling Benkei's attempt to capture the last sword.

Benkei decided that he had finally met a man worthy of the samurai title. Resolved to serve Yoshitsune, Benkei became his devoted disciple. Many gallant deeds are attributed to the two men, and their adventures are the source of many Japanese children's stories about idealism and loyalty.

Despite his youth, Yoshitsune also proved to be a military genius in the revolt that his older half-brother Minamoto Yoritomo eventually raised against the dictatorship of their father's murderer, Taira Kiyomori. Provided with an army by Yoritomo, Yoshitsune was ordered to advance against the forces of his cousin Minamoto Yoshinaka, who threatened Yoritomo's plan for domination of Japan. After a decisive victory, Yoshitsune and his troops occupied Kyoto. He then attacked the remaining Taira forces along the Inland Sea, annihilating them in the famous naval battle of Dannoura during the spring of 1184.

With his base in Kyoto, Yoshitsune became a favorite of Emperor Go-Shirakawa and his court, which aroused Yoritomo's suspicions

Figure 72. Another rendering of the legendary fight between Minamoto Yoshitsune and Benkei on the *Gojōbashi.*

and fear of an eventual political rival. When Yoshitsune attempted to visit his half-brother in Kamakura, where Yoritomo had established his new military headquarters, Yoshitsune was rebuffed with a letter accusing him with having taken arbitrary actions during his campaigns. Yoshitsune then attempted to raise a rebellion with the aid of his uncle Minamoto Yukiie, but was forced to flee after failing.

Hunted by Yoritomo's soldiers, Yoshitsune wandered Japan for several years, often in various disguises. It was during this period that a tessen once again saved his life. This time, though, the tessen was in the hands of his faithful follower, Benkei.

Since the third century, Japan had been divided into a system of *sekisho* or barriers. Originally established for defending the country from the northern barbarians, the military rulers also found them extremely useful for controlling the population and preventing revolts. Any traveler was strictly inspected before being allowed to pass the many checkpoints. Samurai were required to carry a travel pass issued by the local daimyō, while merchants and other commoners had to have a certificate issued by their guild or landlord. A Buddhist priest would be carefully searched in case he was a samurai in disguise as was often the case. Actors, wrestlers, and monkey trainers were the only ones allowed free passage at the checkpoints.

Benkei was disguised as an itinerant priest accompanied by Yoshitsune dressed as his poor servant when they were stopped at the Ataka-no Seki (barrier station of Ataka). One of Yoritomo's agents, Togashi, thought he recognized the servant as the fugitive Yoshitsune and started to interrogate the pair. Thinking quickly, Benkei began disciplining his servant by severely beating Yoshitsune on his head with a tessen. Believing that no retainer would dare treat his master in such a terribly harsh manner, Togashi's suspicions were quelled and he let the two pass unhampered through the barrier station.

Yoshitsune finally took refuge with a powerful and independent lord in far northern Japan, where he lived in relative safety for several years. He was later betrayed by the lord's heir, though, whose troops eventually forced Yoshitsune to commit suicide. After ingeniously aiding his master in many battles, Benkei is said to have died defending Yoshitsune. Pierced with many arrows, Benkei's body reportedly remained standing erect, even after his death.

Japanese Etiquette

When entering a house or room of a senior ranking person, according to Japanese convention, one was to kneel in a special seated position called *seiza*. Seiza is the Japanese style of formal sitting, kneeling with the buttocks on the heels of the feet. The person would then place their sensu a short distance in front of and perpendicular to the knees. Then putting both hands flat on the tatami

Figure 73. Two samurai perform a ritual bow of greeting from the seated or *seiza* position in this Meiji Era postcard.

(woven straw flooring), with the fingertips just short of the sensu, a bow was performed, the depth relative to the rank of the visitor and the host. Figure 73 is a photograph of two samurai performing the ritual of greeting bows.

This common practice is the source for another infamous and very bizarre episode of tessen-jutsu involving one of Japan's famous personalities, Oda Nobunaga. A Japanese warrior and member of the Fujiwara family, Nobunaga overthrew the Ashikaga shōgunate and ended a long period of feudal wars by unifying half of Japan's provinces under his rule. As virtual dictator, Nobunaga restored stable government and established the conditions that eventually led to the unification of the country under Tokugawa Ieyasu.

Nobunaga was born Oda Kippōshi, the second son of Oda Nobuhide, a minor lord, in 1508. He rose from an obscure family to become one of the most powerful men in Japan. One of the most significant steps that Nobunaga took in unifying the country was the destruction of the Buddhist monastery of Mount Hiei. Viewing Mt. Hiei as a threat to political stability, he destroyed the monastery and hunted down every single Hiei monk and slaughtered him, regardless of his age or innocence. Nobunaga was assassinated by Akechi Mitsuhide in 1582.

Known for being stout-hearted, audacious, and autocratic, Nobunaga was reputed to have a quick temper. He was notorious for his unsympathetic and unforgiving treatment of subordinates who displeased him, and was ruthless to his enemies. Nobunaga's punishments for any infraction among his retainers, no matter how minor, were also frequently severe.

When summoned to appear before his lord Nobunaga for some fault, therefore, Akira Murashige knew his life was on the line. With the approval of their lord, Nobunaga's retainers planned to ambush him during his initial greeting. They arranged for the audience to occur with Nobunaga seated in one room and Murashige in an adjoining room.

The two rooms were separated by heavy wooden sliding doors. Several retainers were hidden on both sides of these doors, prepared to crush Murashige's neck between the sliding doors when he performed the ritual bow of greeting.

By chance or by instinct, though, Murashige placed his tessen in the sliding wooden door's floor groove as he made his seated bow. When the retainers slammed the doors together, the doors bounced harmlessly off the fan's iron ribs caught in the floor groove, sparing Murashige's neck. When Murashige acted as though nothing out of the ordinary had happened, Nobunaga relented and spared the official from any further penalty.

A similar incident is reported to have happened between Araki Mataemon, a fencing master, and an unidentified daimyō. However, this may have been an embellishment inspired by the initial incident between Nobunaga and Murashige.

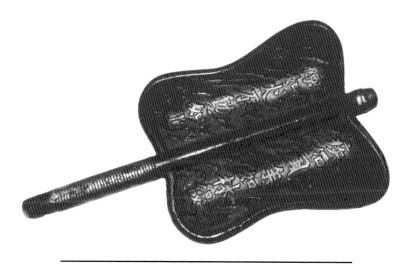

Figure 74. The *gunbei-uchiwa*, a solid fan of either metal or wood. This example is solid iron. It was used mainly by samurai military leaders to signal orders to their troops on the battlefield.

Tessen Origins

The origins of the tessen are to be found among early Chinese influences. This was most certainly the source of first fans carried by nobles in the Japanese court. However, the forerunner of the tessen, the *gunbei-uchiwa*, was a solid, flat fan used by military officers to signal orders to their troops on the battlefield. The early Japanese gunbei-uchiwa were made of either iron or (more commonly) of wood and often featured the leader's *mon* or clan symbol. Figure 74 is a gunbei-uchiwa made of solid iron.

The samurai generals would raise a gunbei-uchiwa above their head, and using predefined motions, communicate battlefield troop movements to their subordinates in the field. Because they were carried by only the highest-ranking officers, as well as being a useful field device for signaling commands, the gunbei-uchiwa quickly became a icon of military authority.

The gunbei-uchiwa played an important role in one of the most famous incidents of single armed combat in Japanese history. One of Japan's most famous generals, Takeda Shingen (also known as Takeda Haruobu), struggled for mastery of the strategic Kanto Plain in central Japan during the civil strife and warfare of the *Sengoku jidai* (warring states period). Born into the powerful Takeda clan, Shingen initially entered the priesthood in 1551. After forcing his father into retirement, though, Shingen assumed the position as head of the Takeda clan and began a long, indecisive struggle to dominate the Kanto Plain.

Figure 75. A sixteenth-century *gunsen*, or folding war fan, shown both open and folded closed. The *gunsen* was frequently carried by samurai in armor and used as a weapon of both attack and defense.

Shingen is also much-celebrated in Japanese drama and folklore for his series of battles with the noted warrior Uesugi Kenshin. Although the battles were relatively indecisive, Shingen was recognized as one of the most powerful warriors in central Japan. As such, he posed a threat to the powerful feudal warrior Oda Nobunaga in his attempt to dominate the central government. Just as the conflict with Nobunaga began, however, Shingen was fatally wounded in battle.

During the fourth battle of Kawanakajima in 1561, Shingen was desperately trying to control his troops from his field command post when, in a surprise dawn attack, a lone mounted samurai burst into the curtained enclosure. According to tradition, the attacker was his archrival, Kenshin, although some accounts indicate it may have actually been one of the Kenshin's leading officers, a samurai named Arakawa. Dressed in full battle armor, Kenshin took advantage of the initial confusion and swung his sword at Shingen, who was seated on his camp stool.

Unable to draw his own sword in time, Takeda Shingen parried the strikes with the gunbei-uchiwa that he held in his hand. According to reports, Shingen took three cuts to his body armor, but parried seven strikes with his war fan before one of his own retainers, armed with a spear, drove off the attacker and his horse.

As an alternative to the gunbei-uchiwa, some military leaders preferred carrying a *gunsen-gata*, the very large folding fan made of iron ribs covered with heavy silk or washi. A thick cord through the kaname allowed these rather large war fans to be secured to rings in the samurai armor's breast plate. Figure 75 shows a sixteenth-century iron gunsen with paper face.

Tessen Decoration

As with other Japanese weapons, many artistic designs were frequently employed in decorating tessen. Often, the outer metal ribs were decorated with either gold or silver inlay or covered in red or black lacquer. Solid metal tessen often featured images of dragons and tigers. Dragons and tigers represent mythical guardians and beneficial forces of nature and are also often found on opposite sides of buildings and temples in ancient oriental architecture.

A sun or moon design was frequently painted on the silk or paper used with the folding styles. The sun and moon in Japan represent *inyō setsu*, the doctrine of yin and yang, primeval forces that mix with each other to create all the myriad universal elements. Solid metal tessen often featured images of dragons and tigers. Originating in China, inyō setsu interprets every thing with a positive-negative opposition like "female-male" or "day-night," while the doctrine of *gogyo setsu* holds that the universe consists of five basic elements—tree, fire, soil, metal, and water—and their transitions. Although initially distinct doctrines, both were eventually merged to form *inyō-gogyo setsu* (inyō-gogyo doctrine) and became popular in Japan during the Asuka period.

Figure 76 shows an Edo-period tenarashi-gata tessen made in the style of a very convincing maiōgi-gata. Figure 77 shows two

Figure 76. This Edo-period *tenarashi-gata tessen* is made in the style of a very convincing *maiōgi-gata*, a fan used in traditional Japanese dancing. As can be seen in the top view, each outer rib has the moon and the sun, signifying *in* and *yo* (Japanese for *yin* and *yang*), cut out to display the underlying gold-washed copper leaves underneath and between the bolstered pieces of russet iron.

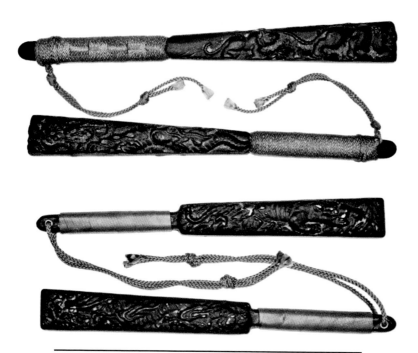

Figure 77. These two Edo-period *tenarashi-gata tessen,* each shown from both sides, are cast of solid iron with a dragon and two tigers on opposite sides representing the mythical guardians and beneficial forces of nature. The one above is in the style of a *sensu-gata* and has a cord-wrapped handle. The one below is in the style of a *gunsen-gata* or military-style fan and has a leather-wrapped *tsuka.*

Edo-period tenarashi-gata tessen cast of solid iron with a dragon and two tigers on opposite sides.

Both the folding and solid styles often incorporated engravings of suitable poems, rank titles, animals or dragons, or other symbolic kanji characters. Sometimes the solid style of tessen would also incorporate a fancy silk cord wrapping as a handle, almost like a bladed weapon. Of course, many tessen were of a more sober and functional style, including little or no decoration of any kind.

Tessen-jutsu

It was considered unseemly for a samurai to use his sword against a lower-ranking rival. On the other hand, tessen-jutsu was considered sophisticated, especially among the higher ranking samurai. Many actually preferred to defend themselves with a tessen, viewing the use of this self-protective weapon as more compassionate than dueling with their potentially lethal blades. Thus, many samurai trained in the defensive use of a tessen and regularly carried one wherever their business or pleasure took them.

As the official kenjutsu school of the Tokugawa shōgunate, the Yagyū Shinkage-ryū is also famous for its iron fan defensive techniques. There are many recorded examples of duels won using iron fans against naked swords and even deaths caused by blows from a tessen. According to one story, a famous sixteenth-century swordsman, Ganryū, armed only with his tessen, quickly defeated several heavily armed opponents.

Tessen-jutsu does not generally constitute separate or individual schools. Usually the numerous kenjutsu-shoryūha (sword schools) and jūjutsu-shoryūha (unarmed fighting schools) would incorporate an assortment of fan or short stick techniques into the other forms presented as part of their particular style. Tessen-jutsu was rarely taught as an individual art by itself. Classical Japanese martial art schools which definitely included tessen defensive techniques as part of their curriculum were Echigo-ryū, Uesugi-ryū, Miyake-Shingan-ryū, and Yagyū-ryū. Of these, only the latter two still exist today in their original lineage and form.

The founder of Yagyū-ryū was Kume Dairanouchi Nagamori, a Sesshu Tsuwano retainer from the area located in modern-day Shimane Prefecture and a remarkable martial artist. Originally trained in the Shinkage-ryū style of kenjutsu, he refined the alternative use of the iron fan as a defensive weapon to prevent unnecessary killing. Due to his desire to never actually cut another man down, the founder created a particular style of Yagyū-ryū tessen-jutsu. Miyake

Seishichi studied the theory of Yagyū-ryū and tessen-jutsu for many years under his Yagyū-ryū instructor, Mori Tanenosuke. As he became older, however, Seishichi permanently lost his eyesight. Since he was now blind, he named his own individually developed style of tessen-jutsu the Miyake-Shingan-ryū, meaning either "spirit eyes style" or "heart eyes style."

Although the practice of tessen-jutsu was considered part of the classical weapon arts, it was primarily intended for self-defense. Tessen-jutsu techniques are based on self-protection rather than intended for more forceful use. Therefore, most tessen-jutsu techniques are designed to incapacitate or restrain an individual opponent rather than to inflict permanent injury or death.

5

Truncheons

The samurai developed their deadly fighting skills on the battlefield as civil wars raged throughout Japan. As soldiers, their weapons were the bow, the sword, the spear, and the arquebus, a matchlock gun introduced by the Portugese. Once Japan was unified and the Tokugawa shōgunate established, the hereditary members of Japan's warrior society gradually lost their military function during the relatively peaceful Edo period. Whether they served one of the many daimyō or as administrators and bureaucrats in the central government, the samurai were now responsible for maintaining social order. As local magistrates and police officers, many samurai were charged with enforcing the law and keeping the peace.

Middle-ranking samurai were called *yoriki*. Their title literally means "assistant" or "helper," although most functioned primarily as general managers and administrators supporting the executive levels of various government offices. Lower ranking samurai called *dōshin* were the uniformed officers and detectives of the feudal era, taking care of the day-to-day business of police work. Several non-samurai assistants accompanied the dōshin as they patrolled their assigned districts. Full-time police assistants recruited from the chōnin population were called *komono*. The komono interrogated witnesses, served as personal guards, conducted surveillance, and ran various other errands at the discretion of the dōshin.

The dōshin depended upon an unofficial network of paid inform-ants and spies to keep them apprised of ongoing criminal activities. Called *okappiki*, these spies were usually from the lowest social classes or outcaste origins—often former outlaws who turned to serving the police to avoid harsh punishments or even execution for their previous offenses. As well as serving as confidential informants and police lookouts, okappiki were chiefly responsible for conducting torture if necessary during criminal interrogations.

Local merchants frequently recruited non-samurai police assis-tants and watchmen to bolster the official police forces. Referred to as *goyōkiki*, these selected chōnin were often local-area gangsters who also worked for the authorities. Some worked as full-time police assistants and security guards, while others were paid as needed, usu-ally to supplement other sources of income. Many of the part-time assistants operated like independent contractors. The goyōkiki were typically responsible for minor policing duties within specific neigh-borhoods. In outlying districts, the goyōkiki (part-time police assis-tants) were also referred to as *meakashi*.

逮捕術
taiho-jutsu

The samurai and their non-samurai assistants employed several unique implements and techniques to arrest and restrain dangerous criminals, who were typically armed and frequently desperate. The martial arts used to capture suspects are generally referred to as *taiho-jutsu* (arresting arts). Many taiho-jutsu methods and weapons originated in the classical Japanese schools of kenjutsu and jujutsu. Unlike the lethal martial arts of the battlefield, though, the purpose of taiho-jutsu was to capture lawbreakers alive and without injury. Thus, the samurai and their non-samurai assistants often used spe-cialized implements and unarmed techniques intended to pacify or disable suspects rather than to kill their opponent.

In the strictly defined society during the Edo period, when class distinctions and the inequality of individuals was an accepted princi-ple, safety and the preservation of life was definitely a major issue when making arrests. Serious injuries inflicted on any suspect might

easily result in chastisement later—especially when arresting someone of higher social rank or status. Therefore, samurai officials and
their assistants always took extra precautions to ensure that suspects
were not injured or killed if at all possible.

There was, however, another reason for police to exercise caution
when arresting suspects. The Tokugawa shōgunate legal system
depended heavily on a criminal's confession as a prerequisite for trial
and punishment. During interrogations, there was always the likeli-
hood the prisoner might provide information leading to other potential suspects and even more arrests. Therefore, the police certainly
preferred capturing criminals alive and still capable of talking about
their illegal ventures.

Jutte

Bladed weapons were dangerous and more likely to seriously injure
or even kill a suspect during a struggle. Furthermore, only samurai
police officers were allowed to carry a sword because of their social
status. Thus both samurai officials and their non-samurai police
assistants relied on a variety of other special implements and techniques to capture criminal violators. One arresting implement that
became a standard for nearly all law enforcement officers was the
jutte, or iron truncheon. In time, the jutte also served as a badge of
office. As the following historical incidents illustrate in graphic
detail, samurai often employed jutte to disarm and arrest suspects.
The incidents also describe the very real potential for injury involved
in such incidents.

jutte

Katsu Kokichi (1802–1850) was an unemployed samurai of little
note for his entire life, although his first son, Katsu Rintarō, later
earned fame as commander of the shōgun's army during the troubled
times near the end of the Edo period. In his memoir, *Musai dokugen*
[Musai's Story], Kokichi provides a rare firsthand account of two
actual arrests, one of a samurai and another of a common gambler.

Both incidents occurred while Kokichi was a teenager and assisting his brother, who held the post of a district administrator.

During a visit to the small village of Sakai to assess the rice crop, Kokichi was asked to help arrest another samurai who injured a local nōmin (farmer) during an attempt to rob the district office:

> *About the same time, a samurai named Sakurai, a kins-*
> *man of Nitta Manjirō in Kōzuke Province, tried to wheedle*
> *some money out of the peasant officials who worked at the*
> *district office. A heated argument broke out, and Sakurai*
> *drew his sword and wounded a peasant. A posse was*
> *rounded up to capture him, but no one dared to go near*
> *Sakurai, who had stationed himself at the office gate and*
> *threatened to slice anyone who came near with his two-foot-*
> *six-inch sword. Several retainers were dispatched from my*
> *brother's office, but they, too, were frightened off and stood*
> *about wringing their hands.*
>
> *My brother said, "Kokichi, go get Sakurai." I ran to the*
> *spot, but with only four feet between Sakurai and the gate,*
> *I realized that it would be impossible to reach him. I would*
> *have to think of something quickly. Just then an outcaste in*
> *the village came up to me and said, "Sir, I have a plan." He*
> *charged at Sakurai with a six-foot pole. The pole was*
> *immediately cut in half, but while Sakurai was still holding*
> *his sword aloft, the outcaste grappled with him. The out-*
> *caste was slashed from his waist to his crotch. In that same*
> *instant I flung a handful of sand into Sakurai's face.*
> *Blinded momentarily, he lurched forward. The outcaste*
> *grabbed him by the testicles and pulled him to the ground.*
> *A couple of other outcastes jumped on Sakurai and bound*
> *him with a rope. He was thrown into the office jail, and fur-*
> *ther negotiations were conducted directly with his kinsman*
> *Nitta in Kōzuke.*

The second incident occurred as they returned to Edo after concluding their business. As was customary when traveling on official business, the district administrator was being carried in a palanquin, a type of litter or sedan chair with latticed sides. After robbing a local brothel, a gambler named Otokichi attempted to secretly join their traveling party by hiding among their horse handlers, apparently in an attempt to avoid detection as the entourage passed through a *sekisho* (barrier station) lining the major highways in Japan. When he noticed the stranger in their midst, though, Kokichi's brother ordered the gambler's arrest:

> *I took an iron truncheon from the side of the palanquin and went looking for him. As soon as he saw me, he broke into a run in the direction of Mount Asama. I chased him, but when I'd finally caught up with him, he put his hand on his long sword and said, "Honorable official, please let me escape."*
>
> *"Let you go? Never!" I edged closer. He drew his sword about a foot, but I noticed that the tip of the scabbard had gotten caught in his rain cape. I immediately hurled myself at him, grabbed the handle of his sword, and turned a somersault. We both tumbled to the ground, with the man landing on top. At the moment, Kitōji, a peasant official from the village of Hiraga, arrived and taking hold of the rascal by the head, turned him over. I shook myself free and gave the man a beating with my truncheon. Kitōji and I tied him up and led him back to the post station at Oiwake.*

The jutte could parry the slash of a razor-sharp sword and aid in disarming a suspect without danger of inflicting any serious injuries. Essentially a defensive or arresting weapon, the length of the jutte required police officers to get extremely close to their intended targets. A jutte could then be used for blocking and parrying strikes

Figure 78. Two feudal police officers attempt to arrest the famous robber Inuzuka Shinao on the roof of the Hō-ryukaku pavilion in this woodblock print by Ichiyusai Kunitoshi. Note the *jutte* held in the standing police officer's right hand, while the fallen officer is attempting to entangle the criminal in chains.

or weapons. A jutte was also useful for striking, thrusting, restraining, and even throwing techniques.

During the Edo period, there were more than thirty martial arts styles that included jutte-jutsu within their curricula. The samurai police officers, called yoriki and dōshin, trained in local dōjōs, often practicing their arresting techniques on komono and okappiki. To effect an arrest, the feudal police were supposed to hold their jutte prominently in front of their faces and announce their intention by shouting, "Go yō! Go yō!" Literally meaning "Official business!," this was roughly the equivalent of stating, "You're under arrest!" They might also admonish the suspect to give themselves up easily with the warning "Shin myō ni hikae orō!" ("Do not run away or try to resist!"). Figure 78 shows two dōshin armed with jutte and other implements while attempting to arrest a criminal.

As low-ranking samurai, dōshin lived on the fringes of proper samurai society. They were often more accustomed to the ways of the lower-class chōnin of Edo. Therefore, it is not surprising that many likely resorted to the simplest and most practical means when arresting dangerous subjects. As illustrated in the firsthand account presented earlier, little concern was often given to ceremonial formalities when dealing with the harsh reality involved in making an arrest.

Figure 79 shows five very basic Edo period iron jutte. The simple functional design and inexpensive construction indicates these were most likely carried by either komono or okappiki. Figure 80 and Figure 81 show several Edo period iron jutte that are larger and better made, and were likely carried by dōshin. Figure 82 and Figure 83 show several more decorative and expensive jutte, probably carried by yoriki.

The remaining jutte found today exhibit many different appearances. The lengths and materials were just as varied as the more decorative accessories. The basic jutte includes a short tsuka (handle) with an attached ring on the hilt called a *kan*. The basic parts and the names of each are shown in Figure 84.

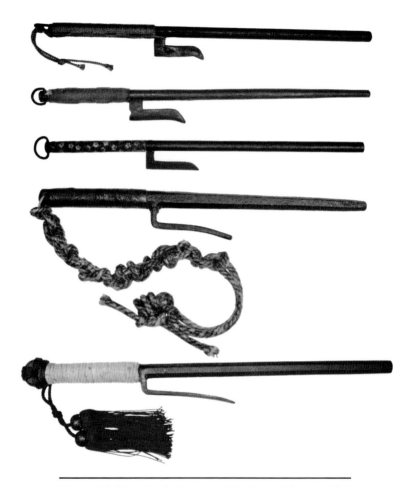

Figure 79. The simple functional design and inexpensive construction indicates these Edo period iron *jutte* were most likely carried by either *komono* or *okappiki*.

In defense against edged weapons such as swords, knives, or even spears, the hexagonal-, octagonal-, or round-shaped boshin (shaft body) was used principally for blocking and parrying techniques. As a metal truncheon, the boshin was also employed primarily for striking the opponent's head or body. The dull, unsharpened shaft tip,

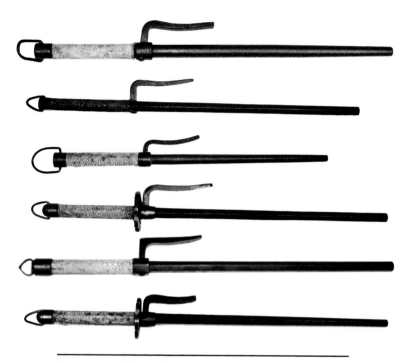

Figure 80. *Dōshin* (low-ranking samurai police officers) likely carried these six Edo period *jutte*.

called a *sentan*, and even the back end of the tsuka were used for various thrusting or stabbing techniques.

Most jutte from this period include a single hook or fork, called a *kagi*, on one side of the boshin near the handle. Some more unusual jutte even have two or more kagi on opposite sides of the shaft. If the kagi is fixed by a hole completely through the boshin, the protrusion on the opposite side is referred to as *kikuza* (chrysanthemum seat). A wood or iron truncheon without any kagi is referred to as *naeshi* or *nayashi*, different kanji characters both meaning "to weaken" or "to paralyze."

There is some disagreement about the actual purpose of the kagi. Many historians claim the hook allowed the jutte to be used for

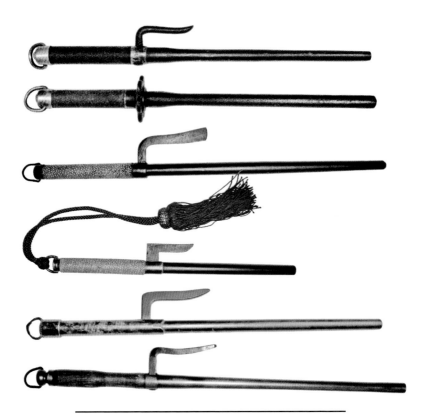

Figure 81. These six Edo period *jutte* were probably carried by *dōshin.*

trapping or even breaking the blades of edged weapons, as well as for jabbing or striking. While the jutte techniques of several classical ryūha use the kagi for this purpose, most still employ the jutte primarily as a truncheon.

Other proponents claim it was too impractical to use the jutte to trap a sword blade, suggesting the kagi was actually a hook to prevent it from slipping through the wearer's obi. The kagi may still have been used to entangle the clothes or fingers of an opponent.

Some jutte, basically simple bars of forged iron, were clearly

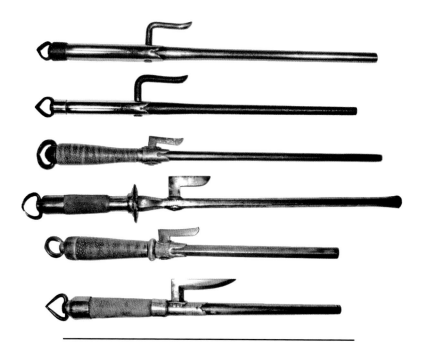

Figure 82. Due to the more extensive decoration, crafts-manship, and use of precious metals, these six Edo period *jutte* were likely carried by high-ranking samurai police officials called *yoriki.*

practical implements. Other jutte are very detailed and include intri-cate designs and decorations. In the latter case, jutte often include tsuka or even tsuba (hand guards) almost identical to sword fittings. Infrequently, jutte may also have incorporated inlaid gold or other precious metals as further decoration.

Highly decorated jutte were most likely more symbolic in nature and an emblem of office rather than intended to be used as an actual self-defense weapon. In this case, the jutte design was intended to impress others and was not necessarily functional. Figure 85 shows two jutte decorated with inlaid silver designs.

But decorative jutte could be functional as well. Figure 86 shows a heavy Edo period jutte cast in solid brass. Despite its decorative

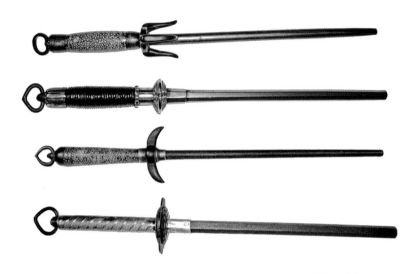

Figure 83. These four Edo period *jutte* are decorative and also have unusual shaped *kagi*. These *jutte* were probably carried by high-ranking samurai police officials (*yoriki*).

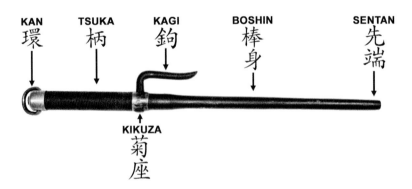

Figure 84. The parts of a typical Japanese *jutte*.

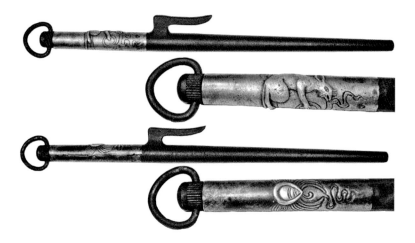

Figure 85. This pair of early Edo-period *jutte* with brass *tsuka* are decorated with inlaid silver designs. The top one includes an inlaid silver rat while the lower one has a *hoju-dama* (flaming jewel). Both also have engraved esoteric Buddhist symbols. These rather small *jutte* with a round tapered *boshin* were likely carried in a special silk bag tucked inside the lapels of a *kimono* worn by a samurai police officer.

Figure 86. This heavy Edo period *jutte* is cast in solid brass with a pine tree, bamboo, and crescent moon in relief along the tapered round *boshin*. Small dents along the *boshin* suggest the *jutte* was used in action at some period.

motif, several small dents along the boshin suggest this jutte was used in action at some period.

The yoriki and dōshin carried their own individual jutte. The dōshin jutte was frequently larger and more substantial. Because the higher-ranking officers only directed or supervised police raids, the yoriki had little practical use for a functional jutte. They often carried much smaller jutte often made of brass as symbols of their status. These were wrapped either in cloth or in special-made silk bags and tucked inside the lapels of their kimono. They were only shown when necessary to indicate the officer was on official business.

Jutte would often have a short cord and tassel tied to the kan on the hilt of the tsuka. Some speculate that the tassel colors indicated the bearer's rank or social position. Because most feudal police jutte were custom-made and privately owned, they were often not subject to official regulations, making it difficult to confirm the colors used or their significance, if any.

However, it is generally assumed that black was used by non-samurai assistants, red for dōshin, and purple for yoriki. Other sources report that regulations specified dōshin use bright reddish-orange tassels, while non-samurai police assistants were not allowed any tassel at all. A white cord and tassel were used by the special police unit in charge of arson and organized robbery, the *hitsuke tōzoku aratame-kata dōshin*. The *hasshu mawari*, patrol officers with jurisdictions over major highways, carried jutte with red tassels. There is also evidence that other color variations, including green and blue, were employed by various offices in different regions. It is also quite possible that the colors of the tassels were changed for different seasons.

While some komono and goyōkiki were occasionally provided with their own individual jutte to carry, very basic jutte were issued on an as-needed basis to other chōnin assistants. The latter were more often very simple and cheaply constructed jutte, since decoration served no real purpose. These jutte were also usually issued for specific duty assignments. When finished with their arresting duties, the komono or goyōkiki were expected to return their jutte to the local police station. Occasionally, komono and goyōkiki were also given their own jutte to mark extraordinary service, such as capturing a dangerous criminal or to recognize their relative status as community leaders.

As paid informants and unofficial police assistants, the okappiki were not legally authorized to carry jutte. Despite this restriction, many komono, goyōkiki, meakashi, and even okappiki had special jutte made at their own expense. The private ownership and personal use of such jutte by both official and unofficial chōnin assistants was apparently tolerated by the machi-bugyō and his officers.

In addition to the feudal Japanese police, other high-ranking samurai also carried jutte as badges of their specific office. For example, the aratame (official inspectors) carried jutte for purposes of identification. These offices included the *yado aratame* (hotel and inn inspectors), *kome aratame* (rice inspectors), and *sakoku aratame* (cereal and other grain inspectors). Since it was highly unlikely the aratame would actually use their jutte for self-defense purposes, they were often more decorative than the more functional ones carried by the police and their assistants. Figure 87 is a highly decorative jutte carried by an aratame as a symbol of his office.

Figure 87. This very decorative *jutte*, most likely from the mid-Bakamatsu period (1853–1868) as indicated by the brass fittings, was probably carried by an *aratame* (official inspector) primarily for identification and as a symbol of office. The *tsuka* and *kagi* are engraved in intricate detail.

Non-samurai police and low-ranking samurai patrol officers typically wore their jutte stuck in their obi on their left hip much like wearing either a wakizashi or tantō. With the jutte stuck in their obi, it could then be drawn quickly with either left or right hand. Not only was the jutte easily accessible, but it also served to display their official status as feudal police officers and government representatives.

If working in disguise on surveillance assignments, they would often conceal their jutte at the back of their obi with the handle pointed to their right side. The jutte would then be hidden under the hanten, a short work coat worn by chōnin, or a haori, a kimono overcoat worn by samurai and wealthy chōnin. Many laborers carried a short workman's knife or other tools tucked safely into their obi at the back, so this would not appear unusual. The jutte could then be easily drawn with the right hand. If their mission was particularly dangerous, they might carry their jutte tucked inside the front of their kimono lapel on the left side, along with a tantō or other arresting implements.

Figure 88. Left: A *jutte* worn tucked in the *obi*. Right: A *jutte* concealed inside the kimono.

Higher-ranking samurai police officers and aratame typically carried their jutte tucked inside the front of their kimono lapel on the left side. The jutte would sometimes be wrapped in a small cloth or even carried in a special silk bag. The officers and official inspectors would usually only draw their jutte for purposes of identification. To pass a checkpoint or guard station, the officer would draw and show his jutte, often just the handle and maybe part of the shaft, to let others know he was currently working on official business. Figure 88 shows two ways of wearing a jutte.

Once drawn, the jutte is typically held firmly in the right hand with the boshin extending as an extension of the hand. In some cases, a short cord and tassel were fixed to the kan at the hilt of the tsuka. Practitioners of certain jutte-jutsu styles then wrapped the cord and tassel around the tsuka near the base of the kagi. Although the purpose was mostly decorative, the fingers were then inserted under the cord loop to secure the grip and prevent losing the weapon during a struggle. Figure 89 shows how to grip a jutte.

Figure 89. The head of Masaki Ryu Manrikigusari-jutsu-ryū, Yumio Nawa *sensei*, demonstrates the proper *jutte* grip and use of the tassel to secure the cord as taught in Edo Machikata Jutte-jutsu-ryū.

Figure 90. When making an arrest, the feudal samurai police officers held their *jutte* over their head.

Figure 91. *Namite* grip (left) and *sakate* grip (right).

Any remaining cord was either looped around the wrist or inter-laced between the fingers. A common method was apparently to grip the jutte with the tassel at the cord end extending between the little and ring fingers of the right hand. In this way, the jutte was secured even when switching grip positions for striking or blocking techniques.

Figure 92. The *kamae* on the left is a non-aggressive stance, while the *kamae* on the right is a more defensive posture.

If thrown at an adversary to distract or wound him, a jutte could then be quickly recovered by retaining hold of either the cord or the tassel.

When making an arrest, the basic grip was generally used. Referred to as *namite*, this grip allowed the boshin and sentan to be pointed at the opponent. The basic grip utilized the weapon as an extension of the hand. The boshin extends from the thumb side as the tsuka is held in the fist. The boshin could then easily be used in blocking, parrying, and striking techniques, while the sentan could be used for thrusting and stabbing techniques.

As an alternative, the weapon could also be held with the boshin parallel with the forearm. In this reverse grip, called *sakate*, the boshin extended from the little finger side of the fist so it almost rests lengthwise against the forearm. In this grip, the boshin was used mainly in blocking, parrying, and holding techniques. Either the sentan or the tsuka pommel could also be used for thrusting techniques.

The basic kamae, or postures, were as diverse as the many styles of jutte-jutsu. Some traditional schools taught different fundamental stances, depending on what type of attack was expected, what type of weapon one was defending against, and whether the defender was seated or standing.

The different kamae ranged from basic defensive standing postures to on-guard positions. Some kamae also varied if using a single jutte or, for example, a combination of jutte and tessen. Figure 92 illustrates two basic kamae used in jutte-jutsu.

Origins of the Jutte

The origins of this Japanese iron truncheon are open to conjecture. Various theories about the jutte have been offered, each with circumstantial supporting evidence. Yet there remains no conclusive information regarding the inspiration for the jutte, leaving experts able only to speculate about the heritage of this peculiar arresting implement.

Hachiwari

Many believe the jutte evolved from a strange battlefield weapon allegedly designed by the renowned Japanese swordsmith Goro Nyudo Masamune. The helmet splitter or helmet crusher, frequently referred to as either *hachiwari* or *kubotowari*, had thick, curved metal blades with unsharpened edges and a hook near the base of the handle. Relatively little is actually known about this unusual implement of war. Worn by warriors like a dirk during the Sengoku period, hachiwari were likely used as a parrying weapon, held in the left hand while wielding a sword in the right hand. Figure 93 shows a Japanese hachiwara from the mid-sixteenth century.

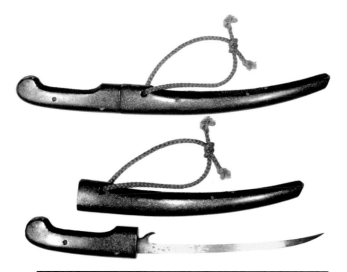

Figure 93. A sixteenth-century *hachiwari* with dark green lacquered *saya* and *tsuka*; several kanji characters are engraved on three sides of the curved square-shaped blade with a sharpened tip and a hook near the base of the handle. One side is signed "*Goro Nyodo Masamune*," a renowned swordsmith and alleged designer of this unique weapon. The other side reads "*Oh-ko Kusunoki Masashige*" (Ordered by Kusunoki Masashige), who was an infamous Japanese general.

Figure 94. These two *tekkan* are made in the shape of *hachiwari* or *kabutowari*. The top example is an Edo period *tekkan* made of steel and including an inlaid bronze decoration. The lower one is a Meiji era cast bronze replica of a *tekkan*, very popular with wealthy merchants and farmers denied by law from carrying or even possessing most types of edged weapons or swords during the Edo period.

The hook may have also been used to catch the cords of an opponent's armor while grappling. Using the leverage of the handle and shaft much like a modern can or bottle opener, the hachiwari hook could then be used to separate armor plates or to tear away a helmet, leaving the opponent vulnerable. The curved and pointed blade was probably designed to pierce unprotected or weak areas of Japanese armor, such as openings just below the arms.

The Japanese *kabuto* (helmets) worn as battlefield armor prior to the Edo period were certainly too sturdy to have been cracked or split open with a relatively lightweight instrument such as the hachiwari. The term, though, may have developed from an earlier battlefield weapon in which iron bars were attached with rope to long wooden poles. When the weapon was swung, the iron bars would strike at the opponents' armored helmets with a hard blow. Iron swords similar in shape to the hachiwari carried during the Edo period were also called *tetsu-ken* or *tekkan*. Figure 94 shows two tekkan.

Sai

Because of the obvious resemblance, many speculate that the jutte evolved from a dagger-like weapon commonly used for self-defense during the fourteenth century in Okinawa. About the length of a wakizashi, the *sai* is sometimes also referred to as a "short sword." However, the sai was basically a short, tapered iron rod with two metal prongs guarding the handle. These unsharpened truncheons were typically used in pairs for stabbing or striking as well as parrying other weapons. The sai could also be rotated on the arm, and the metal handle used for close-range strikes. Some practitioners carried a third sai to be used as a throwing weapon.

Many claim the sai developed in Okinawa from farming implements, suggesting these may have originally been used as pitchforks or plowing tools. It is much more likely, though, that the sai followed the path of Buddhism as it migrated from India and China to the islands of Okinawa. A nearly identical Chinese weapon called a *chai* was designed in the image of the human body by monks who carried them for protection during medieval times.

Chinese Influences

The Japanese jutte may also have roots in the Asian mainland. The *tie chi* (iron ruler) originated in ancient China. A simple flat or round metal rod, this iron ruler was commonly carried by Chinese police officials around the sixth century. The iron ruler was sometimes tapered and even occasionally included a separate handle.

The early Chinese also developed the *bian gan* (whip rod) or *ying bian* (hard whip), hard wooden or metal staffs approximately the same length as a sword. Because they were not sharp and had little potential to cause mortal injuries, these were often used by ancient Chinese police forces to subdue criminals. A very similar weapon, called an *uchiharai jutte*, became popular in Japan near the end of the Sengoku period. These wooden or bamboo hand sticks were also referred to as *tettō*. The metal whip, often in the shape of a bamboo

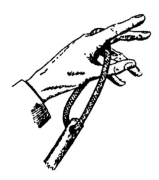

Figure 95. This illustration shows the application of a twitch. (*Veterinary Notes for Horse Owners: A Manual of Horse Medicine and Surgery*)

horsewhip, was referred to as a *kanemuchi*. Possibly because of its effectiveness, the kanemuchi remained popular with higher-ranking samurai officials throughout the Edo period.

Hana-neji

The most plausible theory, however, is that the jutte evolved from an implement originally used to subdue restless horses. This tool was known in Japan as a *hana-neji* (nose screw) and is almost identical to the twitch used today by equestrians. The twitch is basically a loop of soft cord attached to the end of a short wooden stick. By inserting the hand through the cord loop and grasping the horse by the muzzle, the upper lip is caught in the loop. The stick is then twisted to pinch the lip, thus distracting the horse's attention. Figure 95 shows how the twitch was applied.

hana-neji

The hana-neji was a humane method of restraining horses that otherwise refused to be shod or clipped or those requiring medical treatment. As one of the *umagoya sangu* (three tools of the stable), the hana-neji was carried by any samurai involved in training or caring for horses and thus became an early symbol of this obligation. Horses, especially those used by mounted warriors, were considered very valuable in ancient Japan. Therefore, only the most trustworthy and dependable retainers would be selected to supervise a clan's stables. The hana-neji may well have been considered an early emblem of such high rank and vital obligation.

Figure 96. The *karakuri-jutte* includes an iron strip attached by a hinge pin so it could be folded, making it easier to carry and conceal. A separate iron strip fits into a slot to lock the hand guard in place when unfolded.

There is also evidence the hana-neji may have been used during earlier periods in capturing horse thieves—logically enough, it being a tool at hand wherever horses were found. Since this unique implement was originally employed to subdue agitated horses and even possibly to restrain captured thieves, it is not difficult to believe it played a part in the eventual development of the jutte used by samurai police officers to apprehend criminals.

Yari-jutte

The term *jutte* is typically used in later references found during the Edo period. It consists of two kanji characters, one representing the number ten and the second representing a hand. Many historians have interpreted this as a reference indicating the jutte gave the user the "power of ten hands." However, it is far more likely the name is based on another unique and curious personal weapon called either a *yari-jutte* or *karakuri-jutte*. Not much information is known about this strange and unusual looking weapon since only a few illustrations and vague historical references remain.

The blade was made like a *yariho* (spearhead) and obviously was intended for stabbing an opponent at close range. Considerably shorter than a yari, the opposite end formed a rough handle for gripping with the left hand. A long thin strip of iron fitted to the hilt provided hand protection, suggesting the implement was likely used as a parrying weapon, held in the left hand while wielding a sword in the right hand, much like the hachiwari.

The hand guard of the yari-jutte was solid and fixed permanently in a cross-like shape. The iron strip on a karakuri-jutte, though, was attached by a hinge pin similar to the kaname of a tessen, thus allowing the weapon to be folded, probably to make it easier to conceal and to carry. A separate iron strip fitted into a slot to lock the hand guard in place when unfolded. Both the yari-jutte and karakuri-jutte often included a sharp pointed kagi, probably for trapping a sword blade or for snagging an opponent's armor lacing. Figure 96 shows a karakuri-jutte open and folded.

The karakuri-jutte was one of the primary military weapons taught in the Jittetōri-ryū, a martial arts style introduced by the father of Japan's most well known swordsman. Miyamoto Musashi traveled extensively throughout Japan's provinces during the early years of the Edo period, where he reputedly challenged and defeated nearly sixty other kenjutsu experts. His original name was Miyamoto Masana, but he was also sometimes known later in life as Niten. The founder of the Nito-ryū (fencing with two swords) martial arts style, Musashi was also an accomplished artist and author of the *Book of Five Rings*, a treatise on the strategy of swordsmanship.

Musashi's father, Miyamoto Munisai, founded a martial arts style known as Jittetōri-ryū. This particular school, sometimes referred to as Tōri-ryū kenjutsu, utilized several military weapons, including both the katana and wakizashi (nitō-ken), the yari, and the karakuri-jutte. Practitioners of Jittetōri-ryū were especially known for their skill in *sōjutsu* (spear arts) employing a jūji-yari-jutsu, a spear with a distinctive cross-shaped blade.

The jūji-yari was so named because the spear blade's shape resembled the kanji character representing the number ten. In much the same way, the cross-like shape of the yari-jutte and karakuri-jutte also look like the kanji character for ten. Since this implement was carried in the hand, it is reasonable to assume this is the basis for the weapon being called a jutte. Although the yari-jutte and karakuri-jutte were used primarily for offense unlike the iron truncheon, both implements were designed to parry an opponent's sword blade. Therefore, the feudal Japanese police truncheon was most likely called jutte after its forerunners, the yari-jutte and karakuri-jutte.

Other Names for Truncheons

Some older martial arts texts use different Japanese kanji characters to describe an iron truncheon. In addition to differences in pronunciation, these terms also have widely different meanings or translations. For example, the initial kanji character used for the term during the Sengoku period represents "truth." Although the pronunciation—"jitte"—sounds nearly the same, the meaning could be interpreted more like "truth hand," possibly a more symbolic reference.

Other textual references with similar sounding terms include:

juttei, jittei—
"ten levers"

juttei, jucchō,
jicchō—
"ten even"

jutte, jutsute—
"art hand"

juttō, jittō—
roughly mean-
ing "ten hits"
or "on target"

Other terms refer to the composition material used or the techniques employed, which often do not sound even remotely like the
word *jutte*. Such terms include:

koppu,
honeono,
kotsukin—
"bone axe"

tebō—
"hold in
both hands"

tetsu-ken,
tekkan—
"iron sword"

tetsu-hoko,
tetsu-boko—
"iron halberd"

tettō—different
kanji characters,
but also meaning
"iron sword"

Uchiharai Jutte

For special circumstances, samurai police officers carried a *uchiharai jutte*, a special long jutte, usually with a tapered six- or eight-sided shaft, as their primary weapon and arresting tool. Nearly the length of a katana, the uchiharai jutte became popular in Japan near the end of the Sengoku period. It was usually carried only during large-scale police raids or for arresting multiple dangerous criminals.

For such situations, the dōshin would usually only wear one short sword in their obi. The dōshin either ground the *ha* (sharpened edge) off their wakizashi or carried special wakizashi forged with extra-thick dull blades. Much like the uchiharai jutte, the short blunted wakizashi were considered more suitable for making arrests, especially within confined spaces. A resisting suspect could easily be stunned and immobilized by a strike without risking a potentially lethal injury as with a sharpened sword. Figure 97 shows two uchihara-jutte.

Figure 97. Uchiharai jutte. The top one is a late Edo period or possibly Meiji era with a hardwood *tsuka* bolstered with iron bands and a plain bronze *tsuba*. The lower one is made of russet iron with a long *tsuka*. The *kagi* is reinforced with a heavy forged round iron collar where it is attached with a forged iron pin through the *boshin*. Nearly the length of a *katana*, the *uchiharai jutte* became popular in Japan near the end of the Sengoku period.

Kanemuchi

When working as guards or escorts, samurai would often brandish a *kanemuchi*, a long metal whip sometimes shaped like a bamboo horsewhip. The kanemuchi varied from little more than a short and thin truncheon-like weapon to those which were several feet long. This relatively lightweight weapon was easy to handle and could be used with lightning speed. Although it would not generally slice an opponent's flesh, the kanemuchi could effortlessly deliver a very painful and potentially lethal blow. Just the whistling sound of the kanemuchi slashing through the air would often be enough to intimidate and frighten all but the most audacious of attackers. Figure 98 shows three samurai officers with one holding a kanemuchi.

Figure 98. This engraved magazine illustration published in 1874 shows three feudal police officers taking a break for refreshment. The samurai in the middle is holding a *kanemuchi* shaped like a long bamboo horsewhip. The two *yoriki* on the left also have *jingasa*, lacquered or iron-plated helmets.

Protection

The Japanese samurai first began wearing battlefield armor near the time of the Gempei War (1181–1185). To protect themselves from arrows, swords, spears, and bullets, early samurai wore upper body armor with suspended shoulder and upper-arm protection plates. The samurai's protective helmet, or kabuto, consisted of several heavy iron plates bolted together. The kabuto was also often elaborately decorated depending on the wearer's rank. While the samurai's armor provided a form of protection during wartime, it was very heavy and quite restricting.

During the Edo period, most samurai would not wear battlefield armor in public except in extremely unusual situations or for very formal occasions. Should they expect an altercation or challenge, though, many samurai instead wore chain-mail undergarments as well as heavy cloth hand and shin wraps with metal strips sewn into the cloth providing protection against sword or knife cuts.

The *kote* (wrist guards) and *sune-ate* (shin guards) were typically made of iron strips or chain mail sewn on top of heavy cloth. The iron parts were often painted or lacquered to prevent oxidation. These could easily be worn underneath street clothing and offered a covert means of protection in case of a confrontation.

Instead of the Japanese kabuto worn on the battlefields to protect their heads from swords and arrows, samurai during the Edo period would often wear a *hachimaki* (head band) with either metal wires sewn between the cloth layers or a metal strip placed strategically over the forehead. The metal strip was referred to as *hachi-gane*. The hachi-gane or wires would provide a minimum of protection against being cut by a direct downward slash to the forehead. The tops of the ears were then bound under the hachimaki to prevent them from being severed by a glancing sword cut.

As an alternative for head protection, lower ranked samurai would often wear a *kuro uroshi hitai ate*, a half-bowl shaped helmet made of iron plates. These were padded with cloth lining called *ukebari* and

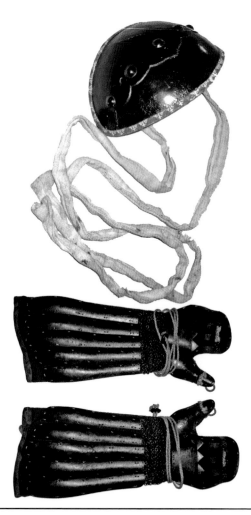

Figure 99. A classic example of the *kuro uroshi hitai ate*. This alternative form of armored head protection includes two iron plate construction with large *o-boshi* rivets. It has an undulating plate edge and pierced circular decorations. The original *ukebari* (padded cotton cloth lining) and stenciled *shobu-gawa* leather trim are intact. The matched cotton cloth tie-cords, *hinobi-no-o*, are period original. The *kote* (wrist and hand guards) are made of iron strips and chain mail sewn on top of heavy blue cloth. The iron strips and chain mail are *urushi* (painted black) to prevent oxidation.

trimmed with leather. The kuro uroshi hitai ate was secured much like the hachi-gane with cloth tie cords called *hinobi-no-o*. Figure 99 shows an Edo period kuro uroshi hitai ate and set of kote with iron strips and chain mail.

In most everyday circumstances, though, Edo period samurai would simply wear a *jingasa*. Made of iron, leather, paper, wood, or bamboo covered with lacquer, jingasa were made in many different shapes and styles. Many were simply round shaped and nearly flat, similar to the conical straw *kasa* (hats) worn by farmers and travelers. Most were colored black and would include a *mon* to distinguish the family or clan relationship.

The inside of the jingasa's shallow top was padded with a *zabuton* (cushion) and included four *ago himo* or rings for attaching cords. The cords were tied tightly around the ears and chin to secure the jingasa to the head. The primary purpose of jingasa was to protect against rain or direct sunlight, although they offered at least a minimum of security against sword slashes as well.

Uke-waza

Samurai were quite adept at using close-range truncheon weapons. To overcome disadvantages inherent to the relative short length and the respective limited effective range, the samurai learned to quickly close with their opponent as well as to employ unarmed grappling expertise for success. Therefore, techniques with such short weapons often incorporated training in various schools of ju-jutsu popular during the feudal era.

The techniques shown in Figure 100 are basic *uke-waza* (blocking techniques) used against an unarmed opponent. In most cases, the same blocks could be used to counter either an opponent's fist strike or kick from either side. The following situations involve blocking an opponent's strike with a fist toward the head. The same techniques could also be used to block strikes with both right or left

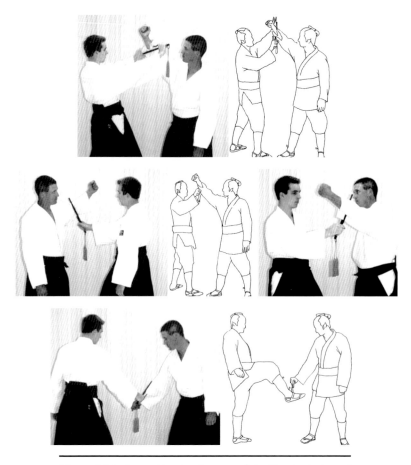

Figure 100. Several basic *uke-waza* (blocking techniques) against an unarmed opponent.

fist or kicks with either foot. Further, the following techniques could be performed as either an inside or outside block by shifting the direction of turn and altering body movement.

Nagashi-waza

Made of either iron or steel, the jutte and tessen were both very effective for defense in blocking and parrying techniques, especially

Figure 101. Several *uke-waza* (blocking techniques) used to parry a sword or other edged weapon.

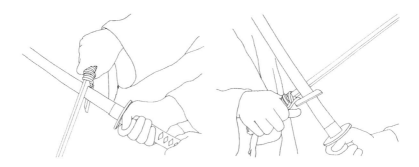

Figure 102. When trapping a bladed weapon with the *kagi*, it is more practical to do so from the back, unsharpened edge of the blade as shown on the left. Several classical *jutte-jutsu* styles include techniques for trapping and breaking the blades of edged weapons as shown on the right.

against edged weapons. If an opponent were armed with a short club or knife, basic blocks could also become effective for *nagashi-waza* (parrying techniques). Instead of blocking the opponent's arm, though, the same block might also be applied to parry the opponent's weapon.

If a longer staff, such as a jō or bō, was used, the techniques used to parry the strike were the same as against the sword. Pressure applied to the side of the opponent's weapon redirects the force of the strike. The techniques shown in Figure 101 are basic uke-waza (blocking techniques) used against an armed opponent.

Many historians claim the kagi allowed the jutte to be used for trapping or even breaking the blades of edged weapons, as well as for jabbing or striking. Several classical jutte-jutsu styles employ the kagi for this purpose. If using the kagi to trap a sword or knife blade, it is more practical to do so from the back, unsharpened edge of the blade. Figure 102 illustrates the use of the kagi to trap a bladed weapon.

Figure 103. An elbow trap against a sword draw: Block the opponent's right elbow with cupped left hand, then point the tip of the weapon toward the opponent's face, forcing his head to go backwards.

Figure 104. A wrist trap against a sword draw: Trap either the opponent's wrist or the sword handle with downward pressure.

The key to an effective parrying technique would be to block an opponent's sword before it is drawn. Against a drawn sword, a parry should be done as close to the tsuba, or hand guard, as possible. Leverage prevents the opponent from executing the full force of the strike. Closing the distance to an opponent rapidly and a certain degree of aggressiveness are good strategies.

Figure 103 shows a technique using an elbow trap as the opponent attempts to draw a sword. Figure 104 illustrates a similar trapping technique applied against the opponent's wrist or sword handle.

Atemi-waza

As with any truncheon, the jutte could be used for a variety of atemi (hitting techniques), both offensive and defensive. These can generally be classed into two major groups. The most common is the slash, or *uchi-waza* (slashing technique), using the boshin, usually against an opponent's joint such as the wrist, elbow, ankle, or knee. The second type of strike is the *tsuki-waza* (thrusting technique). In this case, the sentan or tsuka pommel is used to jab an opponent's sensitive areas such as the throat, solar plexus, face, head, or nerve points. A tremendous amount of force can be generated with either type of

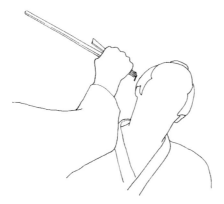

Figure 105. The pommel of the *tsuka* can also be used for striking.

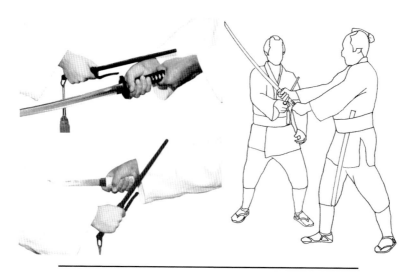

Figure 106. Several typical *uchi-waza* (slashing techniques) against an armed opponent.

strike, sufficient to cause severe pain and even break bones. The jutte can thus be used for either painful strikes to soft-tissue areas or disabling blows to an opponent's kyūsho (vital points). Figure 105 shows a tsuka pommel used for striking.

Students of kenjutsu are taught to hold their sword with both hands with a relaxed grip, much as if cradling a small child in their arms. The sword is swung overhead with the left hand at the hilt providing speed and power and the right hand near the tsuba controlling the direction and angle of the blade for the final cut. Just prior to impact with the target, the hands are twisted inward on the tsuka, much as if wringing a wet towel between both hands. This action both tenses the muscles and properly aligns the bones of the wrist joints directly behind the force of the impact. When the sword is swung in an arc, the last few inches of the blade travel the greatest distance and therefore move faster than any other part of the sword. The wringing action of the wrists and hands provides a sort

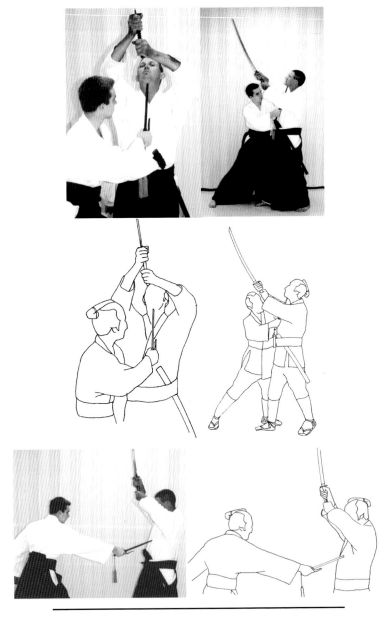

Figure 107. Several typical *tsuki-waza* (thrusting techniques) against an armed opponent.

of snapping motion at the last possible instant, adding speed and power just as the blade tip cuts into the target.

Of course, it is possible to use a jutte like a cudgel or stick and strike an opponent with simple overhand blows. In much the same way as the sword, though, the effectiveness of any truncheon strike or block can be significantly enhanced with the application of relatively simple techniques.

First, the speed of the boshin can be improved by taking advantage of centrifugal force in one of two ways. For large strikes, the truncheon can be swung in a large circle, similar to the cutting action of a sword. When it is impractical or impossible to use an overhand strike, the wrist can be rolled, drawing a circle in the air with the sentan just before striking the target. This rolling action, referred to as *maki-uchi* (rolling inside), can be used to swing the sentan in a circular direction to strike or block from either inside, outside, above, or below the arm. Figure 106 shows several typical uchi-waza (slashing techniques) against an armed opponent.

Obviously, a short baton-like implement such as the jutte is typically held in one hand, yet a wringing action similar to using both hands in sword cuts can still be employed. It is important to maintain a relaxed grip until the instant before impact. Tensing the muscles, combined with a sort of snapping motion from the elbow and a twisting or wringing motion at the wrist, adds even greater speed and power to the final blow. When one uses the wrist for added leverage in this type of slashing strike or block, the boshin can be swung with great speed for a very sharp impact.

Simultaneous blocks and strikes to the arm muscles can immobilize the limb, breaking an opponent's hold or forcing him to drop a weapon. Bicep, tricep, brachial artery on the inside of the bicep, and the inner and lower sides of the forearm are all highly effective target strikes. A sharp strike to any bony area would generally discourage most assailants. A harder, well-placed blow could easily break bones.

When used for thrusts, the sentan or the tsuka pommel concentrate the force of a strike into a single point. Thrusting the jutte into an attacker's leg can instantly deter any kicks. The opponent's thigh, shin, and calf are all potential targets. Stabbing into the femoral artery high on the inner thigh near the opponent's groin can collapse a leg very quickly for a takedown. Figure 107 shows several typical tsuki-waza (thrusting techniques) against an armed opponent.

Muscle strikes can cause deep bruising and temporary loss of use to an opponent's limb. Strikes or thrusts aimed at the front or back of the upper body could deter an attack. A hard thrust with the jutte to the opponent's kidneys, ribs, or sternum would stop most attackers and may also damage internal organs. Potentially lethal targets include an adversary's eyes, temples, throat, and the base of the skull.

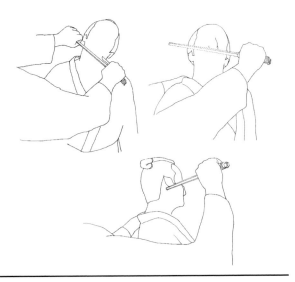

Figure 108. Pressing into nerve points such as the mastoid (cavity behind the ear), philtrum (base of nose), and jugular notch (base of windpipe) are effective methods for controlling an opponent.

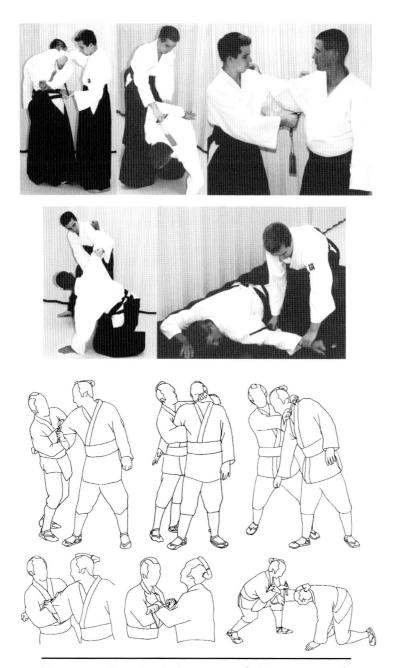

Figure 109. Several typical *osae-waza* (holding techniques).

Osae-waza

The jutte could be used in *osae-waza* (holding techniques) to restrain or immobilize an opponent, as well as to gain compliance from an unwilling subject. If necessary to control an unruly adversary, the jutte offered added leverage to augment holding, joint-locking, and strangulation techniques, making it effective to gain compliance or to subdue an unwilling subject. An opponent's wrists, arms, and legs can be easily locked, controlling even the largest opponent by using the leverage and pain created by the jutte to immobilize an adversary's limbs.

In addition to striking and stabbing, the jutte was also very effective for applying compliance techniques against reluctant subjects. The jutte could be used in a variety of painful techniques. Control is maintained as long as the technique is applied but has no lasting effects when released. This made the jutte a very effective instrument when the primary goal was subject compliance rather than permanent injury.

The sentan or boshin pressed into nerve points such as the mastoid (cavity behind the ear), philtrum (base of nose), and jugular notch (base of windpipe) was an effective method for controlling an opponent. Other sensitive areas included an opponent's earlobe, sternum bone, nostrils, and so on. These points could be attacked from front or rear. If an attacker has seized an individual, the hold could also be broken by pressing the jutte into any of the nerve points that can be reached. Figure 108 illustrates several of these restraining techniques.

The boshin could be employed to clamp either the radius and ulna bones of the wrist or the fingers and thumbs. It could also be used to press down on the back of an opponent's neck or limbs from above to pin and restrain him. Pressing the sentan into the back of an adversary's hand or top of the foot also aids in control. Locking an opponent's anklebone or shins with the jutte was also effective for a takedown or controlling technique. Figure 109 shows several forms of osae-waza used to restrain an opponent.

Shime-waza

For added leverage, the jutte can be used for shime-waza (strangulation techniques). The inflexibility of the metal boshin served to increase pressure when applying either a choke or joint lock, making the respective technique more effective as well as more resistant to any escape efforts. Figure 110 shows several shime-waza used to restrain an opponent.

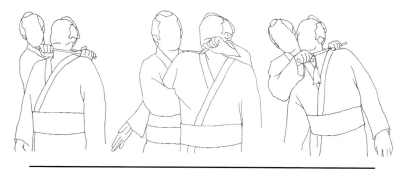

Figure 110. Several typical *shime-waza* (strangulation techniques).

6

Polearms

W hile hand weapons might be used by a samurai to grapple with an opponent at close range, weapons with a longer reach provided distinct advantages. Confronting an opponent could be a harrowing encounter. The samurai often relied on polearm weapons that could be used against a violent opponent from a safer distance.

Polearm weapons were developed from simple wooden implements first employed on the battlefield or to protect homes and families. Before man learned to craft metal weapons, he used sturdy sticks to defend himself, to hunt and kill animals for food, and to wage war against other tribes. Wooden staffs made from simple tree branches and heavy stones found on the ground were probably the first weapons used by one man against another. Later, as metallurgical advances provided the means and men learned to forge knives and swords from copper, iron, and steel, such metal weapons were still extremely expensive and beyond most people's resources.

Polearm weapons played a significant part throughout Japan's turbulent civil wars. As frontline weapons in the hands of the common *ashigaru* (foot soldier), such long arms were essential to keep invaders at bay. Their length often prevented opponents from breaking through defensive battle lines and provided some degree of protection to those wielding them. More important, they were cheap and fairly easy to produce in great quantities for quickly arming peasant warriors.

Long weapons provided the soldier with major advantages over warriors armed with short weapons. The longer weapon offered greater killing potential because of the power inherent in a longer and heavier weapon. Furthermore, the long weapon offered a strategic advantage because it could be engaged well before a short weapon became effective.

Halberds

Halberds such as the nagimaki gave the ashigaru the capability to defend against charging cavalry troops. The heavy blade mounted on a long sturdy wooden pole could be used to cut the horses' legs out from under them, downing their mounted samurai so they could be more easily dispatched with hand weapons. Figure 111 shows a member of the Forty-seven Rōnin armed with a nagimaki as they stormed Kira's mansion.

A smaller and lighter blade mounted on a shorter wooden pole was called the naginata. Because the naginata was more effective in confined spaces, it eventually became the preferred weapon for defense of the samurai household. Even today, many Japanese women practice naginata-jutsu from a young age. Figure 112 is an artist's drawing of a female samurai armed with a naginata preparing to defend her home from intruders.

Yari

The long spear called a *yari*, relatively inexpensive to manufacture compared with bows and swords, provided the common foot soldier with an extremely effective battlefield weapon. Basically, the yari was a metal spearhead mounted on a long wooden pole. Less effort and

Figure 111. A woodblock print by Kuniyōshi shows one of the Forty-seven *Rōnin* armed with a *nagimaki* as they stormed Kira's mansion for revenge.

Figure 112. A samurai woman armed with a *naginata* prepares to defend against intruders in a woodblock print by Kuniyōshi.

material were needed to make and mount each spearhead, making it possible to cheaply produce yari in great quantities. Used mostly as a thrusting weapon, the yari did not require frequent sharpening as did the edge of a long blade. Figure 113 is a woodblock print of one of the Forty-seven Rōnin armed with a yari.

Figure 113. One of the Forty-seven *Rōnin* thrusts with his battlefield *yari* in this woodblock print by Kuniyōshi.

Because it was fairly simple to use, soldiers required significantly less training to develop basic competency, an important consideration when dealing with mostly peasant conscripts. Because of the advantages the length of the weapon offered, many samurai preferred the yari over shorter arms. Figure 114 is an illustration of

Figure 114. Oishi Kuranosuke, the former chief councilor for the disbanded Ako clan, is armed with a *yari* and beating a drum to signal his troops during the attack on Kira's mansion in this woodblock print by Kuniyōshi.

Figure 115. Shorter than a battlefield *yari*, polearms such as this late-Edo-period *teyari* were more effective in confined spaces.

Oishi Kuranosuke, the former chief councilor for the disbanded Ako clan, armed with a yari and beating a drum to signal his troops during the attack on Kira's mansion.

Although ideal for the battlefield, the yari was too long and unwieldy to be useful in confined spaces. The long staff of the yari also made it inconvenient to carry when walking or riding through narrow town streets. Therefore, a much shorter version, called *teyari* (hand spear), eventually proved more popular with samurai during the Edo period. Figure 115 shows a typical teyari.

Yori-bō

The yori-bō (wooden staff), often referred to as a rokushakubō or more simply as a bō, was basically just a long staff made from very hard wood. *Rokushaku* means six shaku and refers to the typical length of the shaft. The length of a rokushakubō shaft would be almost 6 feet (182 centimeters). Although there was no metal blade mounted on either end, the bō was often used on the battlefield by farmers drafted from the fields to fight wars during the feudal period.

During the Sengoku period, the bō was frequently employed by lower-class bushi and ashigaru in the many civil wars and battles that raged all over the country. With metal weapons unavailable either because of their expense or later because of Edo-period prohibitions against ownership, commoners also often relied on the simple bō for self-defense. The bō was used both by nōmin (farmers) to protect their fields and by chōnin to defend their towns from brigands and other invaders.

The most common use for the bō was in striking techniques. It could also be used quite effectively for thrusting or stabbing techniques, especially if one end of the shaft was tapered. Against edged weapons or another bō, the hard wooden shaft could be used in various blocking and parrying defensive techniques.

The bō were often decorated with unit designations or even a family mon (family or clan symbol). In many cases, these markings were burned into the shaft with metal stamps. Some bō were even brightly painted or lacquered.

The bō often varied in length and weight, depending on personal preferences. The typical bō was about six shaku, or nearly six feet long. The shafts were of many different shapes—round, oval, six-sided, or eight-sided—and thicknesses. In some cases, steel or iron rods were hidden inside the wooden shaft or metal strips were attached to the sides of the shaft to provide extra weight and strength.

Regular practice with the bō was often mandatory for rural militia members even in times of peace. Although it had no sharp edges or points, either end of the bō could be used much like a yari or sword. Many martial arts schools specializing in bō techniques existed during the Edo period.

Jō

According to legend, a shorter version of the bō was developed by Muso Gonnosuke Katsuyoshi after losing a duel with Miyamoto Musashi, the famous Japanese swordsman, during the early seventeenth century. Armed with a standard-length bō made of thick oak, Gonnosuke is commonly believed to have defeated many opponents.

Eventually Gonnosuke challenged Musashi to a match. However, Musashi blocked Gonnosuke's attack, hitting him on the head with one of his wooden swords. Most historians believe the first duel between Musashi and Gonnosuke occurred sometime about 1610. According to some accounts, Musashi was whittling either a willow or mulberry branch into a bow. This is supposedly the weapon he used to defeat Gonnosuke.

Humiliated by the defeat, Gonnosuke went into seclusion in the rugged terrain on the southern island of Kyushu, enduring rigid discipline and austere meditation in an attempt to discover a way to defeat Musashi's sword technique. Gonnosuke came to consider the bō too cumbersome and slow. Sometime later, a mystical youth reportedly appeared in a divinely inspired dream, instructing him to create a shorter, lighter bō with a smaller diameter. Gonnosuke called the new wooden staff a jō.

Less awkward than the bō, the shorter jō allowed a practitioner to focus on basic blocking and striking techniques. Because of the reduced weight and length, the jō could be maneuvered with greater speed and flexibility than the bō. After training and perfecting his style, Gonnosuke met Musashi again. The second encounter allegedly occurred on the island of Kyushu, probably a few years after the first confrontation. By this time, Musashi was in the service of the Hosakawa clan. Some claim that Musashi and Gonnosuke attacked each other at the exact same moment, stopping just before striking each other. Realizing they would have both died if they had connected with their individual strikes, the two opponents agreed that their match ended in a draw. After their second confrontation, Gonnosuke accepted a position teaching martial arts for the Kuroda clan, and founded Shintō Musō-ryū based on the jō techniques.

The techniques of using the bō or the jō, often called bōjutsu and jōjutsu, respectively, are patterned largely on traditional sword techniques. The strikes, postures, and parries with the staff closely resemble methods seen in classical kenjutsu since it was primarily intended for use against a sword. As polearm weapons, though, both the bō and the jō effectively combine the thrusts, sweeps, attacks, and parries of the yari and naginata as well.

Wooden staffs were a convenient and common weapon used by *yōjimbō*. These were private security guards and bodyguards from the lower bushi class, or else rōnin, who were frequently employed by wealthy merchants and other chōnin to protect them and their families from street vandals and common robbers. Many of the

Figure 116. As illustrated in this woodblock print, a Meiji era police officer uses his skills in *jōjutsu* to parry the slash of a samurai's sword. Japanese riot policemen still today use *jō* to control angry crowds.

upper-class samurai also employed yōjimbō as household sentries, and they could be frequently seen guarding the gates to their expensive manors with wooden staff in hand.

The Japanese police officers in Tokyo still carry a jō and train in jōjutsu to restrain and control crowds in case of riots. Figure 116 shows a woodblock print of a Meiji era policeman using a jō to parry the slash of a samurai's sword.

Hanbō

An even shorter wooden staff called the *hanbō* (walking stick) was also developed as a defensive and arresting weapon among law enforcement officials during the late nineteenth century. The hanbō was typically three shaku, or nearly three feet long. Because of the short length, the hanbō was also quite useful as a walking stick.

Both the jō and the hanbō were frequently employed as weapons for both personal defense by low-ranking samurai and chōnin throughout the Edo period. Self-defense techniques using the hanbō were especially popular with the general public during the Meiji era, when the samurai class was eliminated and the wearing of swords prohibited. Japanese craftsmen were quite ingenious and found many ways to hide sword blades within otherwise normal-looking walking sticks. Despite prohibitions against openly wearing their swords, many former samurai still carried such sword canes for self-defense. The yakuza and other members of the criminal classes also found such hibuki (hidden weapons) to be quite practical for their illegal purposes.

Arresting Implements

Samurai police during the Edo period used a variety of polearm arresting implements to immobilize and capture suspects without causing lethal injuries. Their standard polearm arresting tools were typically combined into a set of three, including the *sodegarami* (sleeve entangler), the *sasumata* (spear fork), and the *tsukubō* (push pole). Referred to as *torimono sandōgu* (three tools of arresting), these long-handled arresting implements were prominently displayed in front of police stations and government offices as well as in front of the many *seki*, or barrier checkpoint stations, located along all the major highways. The torimono sandōgu were also carried in front of many processions, especially when prisoners were paraded through the streets on their way to the execution grounds. Figure 117 is an illustration of these three polearm arresting implements.

Each feudal police station or guardhouse was required to maintain a set of these long-handled arresting implements in case of any public disturbance. In the hands of a skilled team, these polearm

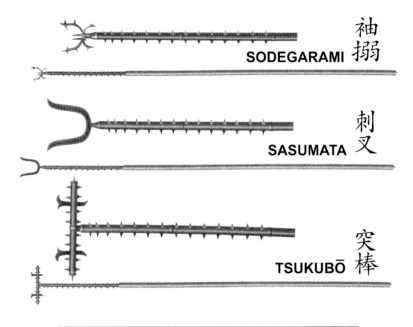

Figure 117. The *torimono sandōgu* included three polearm arresting implements.

arresting implements could easily keep even the most violent adversary at bay. Until the offender was immobilized, the long poles also provided the strategic advantage of protecting officers from the slashes of the shorter sword blade or knife.

The poles were made from very hard woods of varying length, usually about six shaku, or nearly 6 feet (182 centimeters). The iron appendages were attached with a nakango (tang) much the same as a yari spearhead is held in a wooden shaft or a wood-core handle is fastened to a sword blade. A long metal tab with a small punched hole is inserted into a hole in one end of the pole and then fixed in place by a wooden or metal pin inserted through the shaft and the hole in the tang.

Metal strips lined with many sharp spines or points were also often attached around one end. Various materials and shapes—round, square, and zigzag-shaped spines—were used in both long and short versions. The sharp metal barbs prevented a subject from grasping the pole with his hands to wrest it from the arresting officer. These barbs could also ensnare a suspect's clothing, allowing the arresting officer to drag him to the ground.

Sodegarami

The most frequently used of the arresting tool set, the sodegarami was a long pole with many kokagi (small hooks) pointing in different directions on one end. The sodegarami was thrust into the opponent's kimono with a twisting motion to entangle the clothing. With the sodegarami caught in the clothing, the arresting officer then trapped his victim by pushing or pulling him to the ground. Once immobilized on the ground, the suspect could be disarmed and restrained.

The very sharp small points on the tip of the sodegarami were typically called tetsu-sankaku (three-sided iron triangles). Sometimes sodegarami were made with thin needle-like spikes, called tetsu-hari (iron needles), or more rarely, a series of saw-blade-shaped hooks.

Figure 118. A *sodegarami*, probably late Edo period, is shown above. The iron appendages were attached with a *tang nakango*. The long metal tab with a small hole is inserted into a hole in one end of the pole and then fixed in place by a metal pin.

Other names for the sodegarami included roga-bō (wolf's fang pole), shishigashira (lion's head), neji (twist), and tōrigarami (grasping hand). Figure 118 is an Edo period sodegarami with close-up views of the kokagi and tetsu-sankaku.

The sodegarami most likely evolved from the yagaramogara, a long pole implement employed by naval forces. When military ships passed alongside another in battle, soldiers on deck used the yagaramogara to catch an enemy vessel's rigging or cloth sails. Once entangled in the rigging, the soldiers could then pull the enemy's ship closer for boarding.

The yagaramogara was likely duplicated in turn from the *lang xian* (wolf brush), a Chinese polearm weapon dating from the Ming Dynasty (1368–1644) that was used to defend against Japanese pirates who frequently raided China's southeast coast. The Chinese wolf brush was constructed from a spearhead, surrounded by branch-like or thorn-like spikes made of bamboo or iron. The sharp spines indicate that the weapon was probably used to stab or prevent an opponent's advance.

Sasumata

Another restraining implement from the torimono sandōgu was called the sasumata, a long pole with a double-tined fork appendage. The U-shaped attachment was used to pin and control a suspect's limbs or neck. Once an arm, leg, or neck was caught in the sasumata, the arresting officer then immobilized his victim by pushing him against a wall or onto the ground until he could be disarmed and restrained.

The sasumata attachment looks very similar to an accessory used to support and stretch strings on a koto, a traditional Japanese musical instrument imported from China during the Nara period. The koto sits horizontally on the floor while notes are controlled by tiny moving bridges called kojikoto set under each cord. The thirteen silk cords are then played with wooden, ivory, or deer horn picks

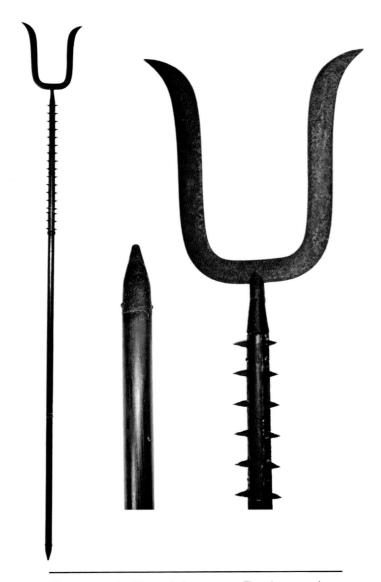

Figure 119. An Edo period *sasumata*. The close-up view of the U-shaped attachment shows a thinner, unsharpened blade. The thin dull-edged blade is lighter and more flexible than *sasumata* used by the professional firefighters. This *sasumata* was probably used by local police officers to restrain and arrest subjects.

worn on the tips of the fingers and thumb. Because the U-shaped attachment looks similar to an upside-down kojikoto, the sasumata was also often referred to as kotoji-bō (koto pillar pole).

Another very similar polearm implement, also frequently referred to as a sasumata, was used primarily by professional hikeshi, or firemen. The fireman's sasumata was used to push down the supporting beams of wooden buildings, either to bring down a burning structure or to create firebreaks. These sasumata were also used to prop up ladders for firemen to climb and determine wind direction and speed.

These firefighting implements were also called chokyakusan (long-leg thing), rinkaku (dragon edge or corner), tetsubashira (iron column), and tokikama (time hook). Because they were used mostly against heavy wooden beams, the fireman's sasumata were made with a thick iron attachment and a heavy rectangular or square-edged shape. The appendage on the sasumata used for arresting purposes, though, was typically shaped like a much thinner, unsharpened blade. The thin dull-edged blade was lighter and more flexible than those used by the hikeshi.

Figure 119 shows an Edo period sasumata probably used by local police officers and their assistants to restrain and arrest subjects. The U-shaped attachment has a thin, unsharpened blade that is too light and flexible for propping up heavy wooden building beams or ladders.

The sasumata is very similar in appearance to another ancient polearm weapon from China, the *chang jiao qian* (long-handled pincers), sometimes also known as huo cha (fire fork) or cha gan (fork staff). This long-handled weapon also had an attachment which looks something like a two-tined fork. Not much is known about the history or techniques of this Chinese polearm weapon other than it was probably used much like the sasumata, that is, to clamp the opponent's weapon, neck, or limbs. It may have also been originally designed for fighting or tending fires.

Figure 120. In this artist's drawing, the feudal police officer in the right foreground uses a *tsukubō* to keep an armed outlaw at bay while the police assistants use a handcart and ladders from the other three sides to help capture the criminal. *(Illustration by Rich Hashimoto)*

Tsukubō

The third arresting implement of the torimono sandōgu was the tsukubō, a long pole with a T-shaped attachment. The tsukubō was used to push, control, and even pin an aggressor. The arresting officer could easily shove and manipulate a suspect with the tsukubō, pinning him against a wall or to the ground. The opponent could also be tripped or pulled off balance with the T-shaped appendage. Figure 120 is an artist's drawing of several feudal Japanese police officers and their assistants using a tsukubō and ladders to arrest a dangerous and armed criminal.

The tsukubō often had sharp metal fingers or barbed spines on the T-shaped crosspiece. These were to prevent an opponent from grabbing the tsukubō or to entangle his clothing. Many of these metal attachments were shaped like a plant or tree leaf with a hole in the middle. If so, these were referred to as *tsukubō-no-you* (leaf of tsukubō).

A rarer form of tsukubō also had two long metal chains with weights attached to each end. These were apparently swung or twirled to entangle the person or his weapons in the chains.

The tsukubō most likely originated as an implement intended mainly for agricultural purposes. The design of the ancient Japanese farming rake was not unlike modern Western-style rakes. Both are basically a wooden rod with pointed wooden or metal fingers. As in most ancient cultures, farmers often trained to use many of their farming tools as arms. The rake doubtlessly proved quite effective as a makeshift weapon for defense against bandits and in the protection of property.

The early farming rakes were made of wood. Later, the rake head was equipped with sharp metal fingers to withstand rigorous use. These were probably the forerunners of the early tsukubō. Other names for tsukubō included teppa (iron fist), hakan (bird wing), getetsuken (moon-shaped sword), saburi (swinging action), and hoko (grabbing hook).

Modern Polearms

Unlike edged weapons, polearm arresting implements and wooden staffs such as the bō and the jō were not intended as lethal weapons but were more suitable for physical control and restraint. This is why the elite Japanese riot police are still required to train regularly with the jō. When called to the scene of a major demonstration or large public disturbance, they are each individually armed with heavy wooden jō and dressed in modern protective gear and helmets.

The regular Japanese police still employ the sasumata as an arresting implement as well, although in a greatly modified form. The attachment on a modern sasumata has a much larger diameter and front opening than the ancient version, allowing it to be used to trap the torso of a suspect rather than the limbs or neck.

Instead of iron, it is made of a hard composite material with large rounded shapes to blunt both ends of the fork and prevent it from piercing the skin or causing any other serious injury. The aluminum shaft sometimes includes two or more telescoping sections, so the modern sasumata is much more portable. When needed, the shaft sections are then extended to their full length and locked in place. Figure 121 shows a modified version of a sasumata used by contemporary Japanese police officers as an arresting implement.

Several years ago, a deranged man armed with a knife walked into an elementary school and viciously attacked several students. Many victims were killed or injured, including several unarmed teachers who attempted to restrain the man. As a result, many Japanese public and private schools have installed emergency sasumata much like fire extinguishers in the school halls and classrooms. The teachers and staff are trained in the use of the updated sasumata to restrain violent individuals. The use of the modified style sasumata allows teachers or staff members to confront and hold someone armed with a short weapon like a knife while maintaining a relatively safe distance. A group of adults armed with several sasumata can easily trap and hold a much stronger person without difficulty.

Figure 121. This is a modified version of a *sasumata*, used by modern Japanese police officers as an arresting implement.

Glossary

Ada-uchi A legal vendetta resulting from a death; also known by the term kataki-uchi.

Aratame A feudal Japanese inspector.

Atemi waza Hitting techniques; the art of striking the vital and vulnerable points of an opponent's body.

Bō A wooden staff approximately six feet long. Also to as yori-bō or rokushakubō.

Bōjutsu The military art of using the bō as a weapon. Bōjutsu is patterned largely on traditional sword techniques.

Bujutsu Military arts.

Bushidō The Japanese samurai's code of ethics, meaning "way of the warrior."

Chōnin The social class consisting of townsmen, craftsmen and artisans.

Daimyō The feudal lords of Japan; each held power over their individual domains, but swore loyalty to the Tokugawa shōgunate.

Daishō A pair of swords, consisting of one long sword (daitō) and a shorter sword (shōtō). Either sword was referred to as katana, although the short sword was sometimes called wakizashi.

Daitō A long sword. See *daishō*.

Dō A Japanese kanji character meaning "way," "path," or "road." Usually a reference to spiritual aspects.

Dōjō A specially designed building or room used for martial arts training. The term means "place to practice the way."

Dōshin Feudal-era police officer.

Eta The term refers to outcasts, or the "non-human" caste, the lowest social class in the rigid feudal Japanese hierarchy.

Fukushū A blood feud.

Fundo-kusari A weighted chain used as a weapon. Literally means "weighted chain."

Go-yō Official business.

Goyōkiki A feudal Japanese police officer's part-time non-samurai assistant.

Gunbei-uchiwa A war fan used for signalling troops on the battlefield.

Gunsen A folding war fan sometimes used as a weapon.

Gunsen-gata War fan style; one of the three standard tessen shapes.

Hachiwari Helmet splitter or helmet crusher; a parrying weapon, perhaps contributing to the origin of the jutte.

Hana-neji Literally means "nose screw." Refers to an implement used for training horses. See *umagoya sangu*.

Hanbō A short wooden staff.

Hibuki Hidden or concealed weapons; also called kakushibuki.

Hinan The lowest social class, considered outcasts.

Hojo-jutsu The art of using ropes to restrain criminals.

Hojokuwa Arresting ring likely used for restraining; this small implement usually had one to four or more short metal points or spikes.

Jicchō A term for jutte meaning "ten even."

Jidai-geki A genre of Japanese television drama which focuses on legends and epic historical events, and in general honors the samurai spirit.

Jingama Camp sickle; the kusurigama evolved from this tool. See also *umagoya sangu*.

Jingasa A special flat lacquered helmet worn by samurai.

Jittei A term for jutte, meaning "truth hand" or "ten lever."

Jō A short wooden staff approximately four feet long.

Jūdo An Olympic sport similar to wrestling. The proper reference is Kodokan Jūdo.

Jūji-yari-jutsu A fighting art using a spear with a cross-shaped blade.

Jūjutsu A generic term for Japanese unarmed fighting styles or self-defense systems. Also referred to as "the gentle art." Other spellings include jujitsu, ju-jitsu, and jiu-jitsu.

Jūjutsu-shoryuha The various Japanese schools of unarmed fighting.

Jutsu A Japanese kanji character meaning "method" or "art."

Jutte An iron truncheon used by feudal-era police officers. Other similar-sounding terms include jicchoh, jitte, jittei, jittoh, jucchoh, jutsute, juttei, and juttoh. Some other references include honeono, kotsukin, teboh, tetsu-ken, tekkan, tetsu-mu, tetsu-hoko, tetsu-boko, and tettoh.

Jutte-jutsu The military art of using the iron truncheon.

Kagi The single hook or fork on the side of a jutte used to capture a sword blade or entangle an opponent's fingers and clothes.

Kamae Stance or posture.

Kanemuchi A long metal whip.

Kanzashi A hair pin worn by Japanese women.

Kappo Resuscitation techniques.

Karasu A tengu which combined human and crow-like characteristics.

Kata Fixed, formal training exercises. Most traditional Japanese fighting arts are centered on these pre-arranged training forms.

Katana Either of the two swords carried by a samurai, but most often used for the longer sword. See *daishō*.

Kenjutsu The military art of swordsmanship.

Kenjutsu-shoryūha The various Japanese schools of swordsmanship.

Kiseru Tobacco pipe, often carried in a case called a kiseruzutsu. Some variations are the truncheon-like kenka kiseru and the large, heavy buyōkiseru.

Kirisutegomen A custom giving samurai the right to kill any member of the common classes who acted other than expected.

Kodokan jūdo A Japanese martial art and sport form founded by Jigaro Kano.

Kogai A kind of skewer carried with the sword.

Kogatana A small auxiliary utility blade carried with the sword, in a slot on the sword's scabbard.

Kome aratame Rice inspectors.

Komono A feudal Japanese police officer's full-time non-samurai assistant.

Komuso Priests of emptiness and nothingness. See *shakuhachi*.

Kongōsho A symbolic item of Buddhism, shaped like a pestle with pointed ends. Types used as hand load weapons include the tokkosho (single-pronged), sankosho (three-pronged), and gokosho (five-pronged).

Kote Wrist. Also the forearm protector worn in kendō.

Kozuka The handle of a kogatana.

Kumiuchi A form of wrestling while wearing armor.

Kusarigama Short sickle with a weighted chain attached.

Kusari-jutsu The military art of using the weighted chain as a weapon.

Kyūsho Vital points on the body; the sensitive nerve centers on an opponent's body.

Machi-bugyō Feudal Japanese combination of town magistrate, judge, and police chief. Their office was referred to as machi-bugyōsho.

Maiōgi-gata Style of fan used in traditional Japanese folk dancing and kabuki; one of the three standard tessen shapes.

Manriki-kusari A weighted chain used as a weapon. Literally means "ten-thousand-power chain."

Menhari-gata Tessen which actually folded.

Metsubushi Sight removers, usually irritating powders or liquids used to distract and confuse an adversary.

Metsuke Spies for the Tokugawa shōgunate.

Mijikimono Small everyday items which are readily available; used as creative weapons.

Mon A clan or family symbol.

Musha-shugyō Meaning "warrior journey," a pilgrimage to obtain spiritual enlightenment through physical effort. To supplement and enhance their martial arts training, Japanese samurai would occasionally wander throughout the countryside to further develop their own skills by matching themselves against worthy opponents.

Mushin A mental state often called "empty mind."

Nagashi-waza Parrying technique.

Nage-waza Throwing technique.

Nagimaki A halberd.

Naginata A halberd-style weapon often used by the samurai. The traditional weapon of samurai women.

Naginata-jutsu The military art of using a halberd.

Namite Basic grip used with the jutte. See *sakate*.

Ninja Non-samurai employed as spies and assassins.

Nitō-ken A style of swordsmanship using two swords.

Nōmin The social class consisting of farmers.

Obi Sash worn around the waist by Japanese men.

Okappiki Unofficial feudal Japanese police assistants and informers.

Osae-waza Restraining or holding technique.

Otokodake Young men who volunteered to help police their community.

Rōnin Literally "wave man," this term refers to an unemployed samurai.

Ryū School or style.

Sai A short, unsharpened truncheon-like weapon.

Sakate Reverse grip used with the jutte. See *namite*.

Sakoku aratame Cereal and other grain inspectors.

Samurai Japan's hereditary warriors and military retainers during feudal times. The term comes from the Japanese verb *saburau*, meaning "service to a noble."

Sasumata Spear fork.

Saya The scabbard for a samurai sword.

Seiza A Japanese style of formal sitting, kneeling with the buttocks on the heels of the feet.

Sekisho Barrier checkpoint stations.

Sensu Basic folding fan.

Sensu-gata Basic folding fan style; one of the three standard tessen shapes.

Seppuku Ritual suicide.

Shakuhachi A bamboo flute.

Shakujo The ring-tipped staff carried by the yamabushi.

Shikomibuki Prepared weapons that appeared to be innocuous everyday objects.

Shikomijo A staff or cane made to conceal a sword blade.

Shime-waza Strangulation technique.

Shinto The Japanese state religion.

Shōgun Japan's first military rulers.

Shōtō A short sword. See *daishō*.

Shuriken A small concealed hand-hidden blade; used for throwing or stabbing. The two basic styles are the bō shuriken and the shaken.

Sodegarami Sleeve entangler.

Sode-kusari A weighted chain used as a weapon. Literally means "sleeve chain."

Sōjutsu Spear arts.

Sun A unit of Japanese measurement, equal to 1.193 inches.

Suntetsu A short metal rod held in the hand and used as a weapon.

Taiho-jutsu A modern form of arresting and restraining art used by the Japanese police.

Tantō Dagger.

Tatami Straw floor mat.

Te Fighting tricks.

Tenarashi-gata Tessen cast in solid iron and shaped like a closed fan.

Tengai Woven basket-like hats worn by the komuso.

Tengu Mythical beings who were supposed to be expert martial artists.

Tenouchi A short wooden or metal object used as a weapon. Literally means "inside the hand."

Tessen Iron fan.

Tessen-jutsu The military art of using the iron fan.

Tobikuchi Firefighter's tool used to tear down burning structures.

Tokin The strange cap worn by yamabushi. It doubled as a drinking cup.

Tori In kata, the person applying the technique. See *uke*.

Torihimo Literally, "bird rope," this was another common term for the short cord used by police assistants to restrain criminals. See *hojo-jutsu*.

Torinawa Arresting ropes.

Tsuba The handguard, usually round, for a samurai sword.

Tsuji-giri Testing a sword blade on a human victim.

Tsuki-waza Thrusting technique.

Tsukubō Push pole; a long-handled arresting implement.

Uchiharai jutte A long jutte used as a samurai police weapon.

Uchi-waza Striking technique.

Uke In kata, the person receiving the technique. See *tori*.

Uke-waza Blocking technique.

Umagoya sangu "Three tools of the stable," including the hana-neji (nose screw), the jingama (camp sickle), and the banshin or umabari (horse needle).

Wakizashi The short sword carried by the samurai. See *daishō*.

Washi Japanese paper.

Yado aratame Hotel and inn inspectors.

Yamabushi Ascetic mountain warriors.

Yari A spear or lance.

Yari-jutte A weapon consisting of a stabbing blade and a cross-shaped hand guard; also called karakuri-jutte.

Yatate Japanese portable writing set.

Yawara A Japanese kanji character meaning "gentleness," "pliability," or "flexibility." This term is frequently used to refer to jujutsu fighting styles. It also refers to a short wooden stick used in jujutsu, also called yawara-bō.

Yōjimbō Private security guards and bodyguards drafted from the lower bushi class or the ronin.

Yori-bō A wooden staff. Often referred to simply as bō.

Yoriki Middle-ranking samurai officers in feudal Japan. The title literally means "assistant" or "helper," although most functioned primarily as general managers and administrators supporting the executive levels of various government offices.

Index